Gifts from an Oak Tree

Gifts from an Oak Tree

A Wisconsin Backwoods Memoir

Kay Moeller Scholtz - Copyright 2016

This memoir is dedicated to my sister and brothers who came before me and lit the kerosene lamps, cut the firewood, carried in the water, stoked the stoves, left home before I did, and made Mom and Dad proud. The majority of material in this book was written in 2013. I've since found the courage to put it in print.

I also write with my heart for my son and daughter-in-law, and my nieces and nephews, hoping to give you a true window into the past and a reason to appreciate the now. You are the ones still lighting the candles for my parents, your Grandparents and Great Grandparents, today. Through you, they live on!

If my words can offer help to someone suffering from low self-esteem from their childhood, personal losses of family members, or those battling chronic or life threatening diseases, then I'd like to share them with the world. Simply knowing that we are not alone, and that life can be good even when it is bad, makes the journey all worthwhile.

PART ONE

The door opens, the light comes on, and I hear him cussing. Dad is home from the tavern. It's late, after midnight, but it's just like every other night. His cigarette smoke fills the air. Dishes are clinking; he's looking for something to eat and stumbles into the kitchen table. I close my eyes tight as I hear every sound through the paper thin walls of our tiny house, and I try to go back to sleep because I have to get up for school in the morning. I don't want to go to school, I hate school. I don't like my Dad. I don't like my home. I can't get back to sleep... and then it's daylight. The alarm clock rings at the foot of my bed and in order to stop it I have to sit up. I put the clock there on purpose so I don't accidentally fall back to sleep again. I get dressed in bed, underneath the covers, because it's so cold. In the kitchen I slug down a bowl of Captain Crunch cereal while I wait for my cherry Pop-Tart to hop out of the toaster. After I finish eating I throw a peanut butter sandwich in a brown paper bag and

grab my school books, lunch bag, and put on my jacket. I run up the driveway to wait for the school bus, listening for its familiar sound while I watch my breath flitter in the cool morning air. I hear the old bus coming around the curve from the north as it always does and when it stops for me with red lights flashing I dash across the highway and climb aboard. Good bye Dad, sleep off your drunk. See you when I get home, maybe... if you're there.

ENTER MY WORLD

I want to share with you what it was like for me growing up in the backwoods of central Wisconsin in the 1960s and 70s, and selfishly I hope writing down my recollections will help me to understand myself and my own past better too. My life at home and our backward ways gave me a severe case of low self-esteem as a child. Although my younger days were filled with tough times, those experiences have made me who I am today.

I have chosen to write about my life just as it was, without any sugar coating or embellishing. What you will read is how it really was for me, as best as I can remember it.

The tar paper shack where I grew up is located on a wooded eighty acre parcel in central Wisconsin. Because of its poor condition it will soon be torn down and only a memory. The land it sits on was purchased by my paternal grandfather, Adam Moeller, in 1923.

The poor lifestyle that encompassed my young world was due in part to my father's love of Pabst Blue Ribbon Beer and also because of his apathetic ways. He was an honest man and a hard worker but lacked motivation at home. I'm still trying to figure Dad out, a World War II veteran like so many of his generation. I think he saw too much. He spent several years in the C.C.C. camps (Civilian Conservation Corps) in Iowa from the age of 16, in about 1933, and then another four years after being drafted into the Army during WWII from 1941 until 1945. I think he became so used to the military lifestyle that he had troubles adjusting to life on the outside. For anything my father did wrong, I have totally forgiven him, because I know he had a good heart.

6

When I reflect on my mother, my heart still overflows with love for that soft hearted, kind, and gentle little woman that she was, not quite five feet tall. I can picture Mom standing in the kitchen with her checkered apron on, frying potatoes and onions in a big cast iron skillet on the old wood cook stove, a hanky in each apron pocket. Or I can still see her watching T.V. soaps, with a needle and thread in her hands, embroidering a pillow case or mending socks. Despite their differences and frailties, I wouldn't trade either one of my parents for any other.

There's another reason I'm writing this memoir and it's because there's a little something that's been playing with my emotions quite a bit lately, and that same something upset my world to no end when I was a kid. I have often called it "The Big C", not wanting to say the word out loud. I'd like to share with others how... cancer... has affected me and come full circle in my life. I hope that confronting it head on, in words plain and simple, will help me handle it better today and tomorrow. I also would like to share with you some of the coping tools I'm learning as I muddle my way through the uncertainties of life on earth. I hope and pray that you never need to use them.

Cancer first knocked on my door with my mother's breast cancer diagnosis back in 1971, when I was 11 years old. It returned again in October of 2012 when I was diagnosed myself with ovarian cancer. I now have a firsthand picture as an adult of what my mother went through over forty years ago, and I often feel that she is still with me on my own cancer journey.

On a recent and first time visit with a psychologist, I was told that my resilience from the past will help me to cope with the future. I hadn't thought much about my resilience until now, or what it really means, but I've taken her statement as a compliment. Finding a way to cope with a life threatening illness is the main key once it grips ahold of you. It can't ever be completely erased from your mind; it's always there once it touches your life. Acceptance is a hard but very important part of the key and I'm constantly working on it.

This is my life... my past and my present... and after admittedly suffering from shyness and low self-esteem through much of it, today I have to say that maybe, just maybe, I am somebody! You see that bit of low self-esteem is still so hard to shake.

I'm standing near the front door of our house with one of my brother's hound dogs in this tattered photo from 1963. Dad built a screen door that closed in front of the house door to keep out the flies and mosquitoes in the summertime. I can see the screen is torn here. We left the front door open in hot weather and the bugs came in. Mom hung sticky fly tapes in the kitchen, thumbtacking them to the ceiling. They were always full. This being one of my favorite photos of myself when I was young, I submitted it for my "baby" picture in my senior high school yearbook.

Here's a photo of Mom and Dad in our front yard taken in about 1970. Grandpa's log cabin home is in the background on the left and my brother, Lynn's, '55 Chevy project car is sitting up there on the hill waiting for his return from the Army. This photo is special to me because I took it when I was about 10 with our little green plastic Imperial Savoy 620 camera. In those days each picture had to count as we often had just a 12 exposure roll of film. Larger rolls were too expensive and took too long to use up. I thought to myself at the time that since we had no current photos of my parents together I should shuffle them out the door in front of Dad's new Ford Futura. Dad was a Ford man.

MY ARRIVAL

I was born in Neillsville, Clark County, Wisconsin, in 1959, at a small city eighteen miles from home. Neillsville is the county seat and had the closest hospital to our home. My dad always said Neillsville was stale because it never grew much in population throughout his lifetime. For over a hundred years the population of Neillsville has been just over 2,000 people. When I was young, despite my dad's negative attitude about the place, I thought Neillsville was a fun city to visit.

My mother said I was three days late in arriving and if I wasn't born soon "they" would have to do something about it! My sister, Marla, oldest of the family, was 11 when I arrived. She has special memories of carrying me into the house when my mother and I came home from the hospital. Mom was in poor health and this pregnancy wasn't good for her. She often told me that she didn't know why she had me, not in a bad way, just that I was a surprise or certainly unintended. I was number seven of her full term babies and there were a few miscarriages in-between the seven.

Mom suffered for years with thyroid problems and had her thyroid removed in the mid-1950s. After my youngest brother was born in 1954, she was told not to have any more children. Five years later when I became the new baby of the family, Mom was soon to be 45 years old. I'm from an old egg!

Springtime in 1963, I'm sitting by a red oak tree just east of our house. A kerosene barrel is on the left and the can and funnel for bringing it into the house to fill up the cooking stove is on the right.

GROWING UP IN THE WOODS

I have few memories of my very early childhood other than those rekindled by looking at old photographs. My first warm and fuzzy thoughts begin with spring time at my Wisconsin forest home. It was a glorious time of year when the cold winters showed signs of retreat. Spring brought hope in the form of warmth, pussy willows, croaking frogs, May flowers, and the return of the robins. It was very exciting when my siblings and I were allowed to run outside for the first time in many months without a coat on and listen to the singing of the frogs in the evenings. In late spring we gathered lightening bugs from our yard and put them in washed out peanut butter or fruit jars. We pounded holes in the jar lid with a hammer and nail so our bugs could "breathe". I took my jar to bed with me and watched the bugs glow under the covers as long as I could stay awake.

I grew up "in the country" thirteen miles from the nearest little town of Pittsville. Our home was built shortly after World War II on land that belonged to my grandfather. Ours was a little stick built home barely big enough for two, let alone a family. There was no foundation under it. The cold wood floor covered with cracked linoleum was propped up on 2 x 4's sitting on the dirt. Strips of black tar paper covered the roof, never any shingles. Fake brick mineral surfaced siding was nailed on the exterior walls. This siding was manufactured cheaply in the 1930s and 40s, and is now referred to as "ghetto brick".

Large sheets of cardboard were tacked to the framed walls on the inside of the house and when I was young they were painted a mint green, like the color of a McDonald's Shamrock Shake. There was no insulation between the walls or in the ceiling in the two rooms of the original house. Makes me say, "Brrrrr…", when I think about it.

Our home was cheap, simple, and very cold in the wintertime. Despite its flaws, my sister reflects how on a winter day when looking at the house from the outside, watching the smoke curl softly out of the chimney and seeing the dim light from the kerosene lamp in the windows, there was something peaceful and homey about it all. I'm glad she felt that way because I don't think I ever did.

Dad had a ritual every spring that I remember clearly. When the frost went out of the ground, everything kind of shifted and settled, including our house. Wisconsin winters can be harsh and Wisconsin springs reveal the havoc they can cause. Things shifted so much that the house door rubbed on the bottom framework so we could barely open or shut it. Dad would calmly get out the handsaw and cut a half inch or more off the bottom of the door so that it would once again open and close smoothly, never minding what the top looked like afterward.

My brothers had their own spring rituals as well. They'd dig out their old fishing tackle, daredevil lures in particular. A small paint brush and some red, white, and black paint would come in handy for touching up the peeling paint on the old lures making them ready again for catching northerns, a real treat at the kitchen table. When finished, their old lures would sport a new coat of either black and white or red and white swirls.

In the summer we contended with flies and mosquitoes in the house and a leaky roof.

For a few years we also put up with rats and flying squirrels in our house. The rats came first when I was about seven years old. I believe they drifted our way from a neighbor's barn. It was hard to sleep at night because the rats were nocturnal and would start having their fun about the time I wanted to go to sleep. They would race up and down the little hallway next to where I slept. Sometimes they'd crawl over my covers while I was in bed. Mom put out poison for them in various places throughout the house and after what seemed like months, they disappeared. One day we smelled something quite ripe and after a bit of investigating we found a dead rat, infested with maggots, in between the sofa cushions in the kitchen. We didn't know what else to do but drag the sofa or davenport as we called it, rat carcass and all, out the door and behind the house. We never got another sofa.

In later years the flying squirrels took over the inside of the house. They were also nocturnal and caused quite a bit of racket in the kitchen where they played with empty tin cans on the floor and crawled inside of them, licking the insides out. My dad was somewhat amused with the squirrels, especially when he was drunk, and never made any effort to get rid of them.

We had no electricity or plumbing when I was born. All of my older siblings and I were raised in that little house. My father moved out of it into a mobile home when I turned 18 and he left the flying squirrels behind. We moved all of his furniture out of the house, a little at a time, and when it was empty he reluctantly headed for the mobile home. Dad was not a man of change.

14

Our little tar paper shack in the woods of central Wisconsin. Dad's '62 Ford Falcon sits out front, after an early winter snow. The cheap siding on the closest part of the house was fake brick tar paper siding mass produced cheaply during and after World War II. Nowadays they call it "ghetto brick". You used to see this siding quite often on little country homes dotting the rural landscape but it is quickly disappearing.

My two oldest brothers finished building the two story addition on the north side of the house when they were 11 and 12 years old in about 1961. They were motivated by the fact that they themselves needed more space. A house with two rooms was no longer big enough for our growing family. If they hadn't finished the addition it wouldn't have gotten done. My oldest brother, Kent, said Dad never pounded a nail.

The window in the peak of the roof let light into the attic but we never used that space for living quarters. There were just a few loose boards up there on the attic floor. My mother stored some of her wedding gifts in the attic and my sister and I found dishes up there still wrapped in their original gift boxes several years after Mom passed away. She never had the opportunity to use or display her "nice things".

GRANDPA ADAM & HIS LOG HOME

Near the home I grew up in, the log cabin built by Grandpa Adam still stands today. It was a grand log home in its younger days, made of aspen (we called it popple) harvested from the nearby woods and chinked with plaster between each log. Grandpa started building the cabin in the 1920s when he purchased the Wisconsin 80 acres in 1923 after losing his Iowa farm. He had cosigned a loan in Jackson County, Iowa, where he was raised, for his youngest brother, Carl, who was irresponsible. Somehow Grandpa ended up with the Wisconsin acreage when he lost the Iowa farm and livestock. He and Grandma and their children (my Dad was the oldest son) moved back and forth from Iowa to Wisconsin several times after losing their Iowa farm. They rented farms here and there trying to make a living, while their family continued to grow. Grandma often suffered from homesickness for her family back in Iowa.

Grandpa moved permanently to Wisconsin after the death of Grandma to pneumonia in 1933, near Maquoketa, Iowa. She was nearly twenty years younger than he was. The youngest of their six living children, Aunt Susan, was just three years old when Grandpa was widowed at the age of 57. With the help of neighbors, Grandpa finished building the Wisconsin log cabin home on his 80 acres. It was a two story cabin with sleeping quarters upstairs for the kids. Grandpa slept downstairs and had a wood heating stove and cook stove in the center. He kept his log cabin neat and tidy and raised his younger children there by himself. Aunt Theresa said their log home was the warmest place she ever lived.

If you look up today at the ceiling downstairs where Grandpa slept you can find a wooden dowel attached between the rafters. Grandpa would use this dowel or rod to do chin-ups. He would pull himself up parallel with the ceiling, legs and all, and do as many chin-ups as his age, when he was well up into his 80s. He also had pieces of wooden lathe tacked together in rectangular shapes and would place them around his chest to measure his chest width. Grandpa practiced deep breathing and felt that a large chest made for better lung capacity and good health. Grandpa was a fan of Bernarr Macfadden, a body builder and health nut, who published a successful magazine in the early 1900s, and sold many books on health, nutrition, and body building.

On the north outside wall of the log cabin was a double door you could open up to walk down into the root cellar. The floor and walls of the cellar were dirt. There were shelves made of boards against the walls for storing jars of canned vegetables. Home grown potatoes, squash, and carrots were also stored in the root cellar. Nothing froze down there in the winter. Grandpa sold his extra potatoes to the neighbors, many returning for more each year as they liked his "medium sized" potatoes better than any others.

One of Grandpa's favorite foods was canned apricots when I was a kid. He would buy large cans of whole apricots with pits inside and kept a good stock on hand at all times. Grandpa would not only eat the fruit but he'd grind up the pits and eat them as well. A ritual that Grandpa had was to place a shot glass of Mogen David grape wine with a slice of cheese near his bed when he went to sleep at night. He would wake up in the night and have the wine and cheese for a snack.

He often wore a knitted stocking cap on his bald head when he went to bed at night. (I can really relate to that now after going through chemo in wintertime in Wisconsin. I have worn a stocking cap to bed like Grandpa too, to keep my bald head warm!)

Grandpa had an antique pump organ that I tried to play although I never accomplished more than reading a few notes and playing with one finger. He always appreciated whatever music I tried to play. I also read to him from newspapers and magazines when I was seven or eight years old. His favorite newspaper comic strip was "Song of the Lazy Farmer". He really enjoyed spending time with my brothers, sister, and I, and our cousins, and we felt the same closeness to him.

17

Grandpa had a log shed, an outhouse, and a jar shed built near his cabin. The jar shed was very intriguing to me. It looked much like the outhouse from the outside but when you opened the door you saw shelves lining the three walls. On those shelves were jars of all kinds, washed and saved with their lids on. There were clear jars, green jars, amber colored jars, and also gallon jugs. By reading the lids you could often tell what the jars had originally held. Some empty jars I remember seeing stacked on the shelves were from Welch's Grape Juice, concentrated lemonade, pickled pig's feet, peanut butter, pickled herring, and pickled pork hocks. There were also many empty Mogen David Wine bottles. If a jar was needed for another purpose, you could usually find the right sized jar in the jar shed. Grandpa knew all about going "green" way back when.

A penciled message written on Grandpa's outhouse door still lingers in my memory. Aunt Theresa wrote it on the inside of the door long ago. It read like this, "Step lightly, step softly, and gently close the door… for many a costly dinner lies buried beneath this floor."

By the time I came along, Grandpa was in his 80s. I have fond memories of Grandpa and his kindness, and the appreciation he showed us for the help and attention we gave to him. As he grew older his vision failed and his knees gave out. He had cataracts but never had surgery to remove them as it wasn't perfected so well back then.

Aunt Theresa cared for him at her home in Illinois during the winter months and then fulltime until his death in 1970 on her birthday. Grandpa was 94 years old when he passed and I was eleven. I'm mentioning the only Grandpa I knew at the beginning of my story simply because his memory is one of the brightest spots of my childhood and I'm sure all my brothers and sister would agree.

Here's Grandpa Adam, in 1966, with two canes and a smile for the camera. His log cabin home sits in the background.
Grandpa was wise, ambitious, and always praising his grandchildren.

SCHOOL DAYS

All of my older brothers and my sister spent at least a few years attending a one room country school called Audubon, about two miles from home. Audubon was the last of four country schools in Sherwood Township where we lived. My sister, the oldest, graduated from 8th grade there and then finished her high school grades in Pittsville. I was the only one in my family who spent all my school days in the village of Pittsville and the only one to attend kindergarten.

Me and my big sister, Marla, at home in 1964

I started kindergarten just after I turned five years old. I was small for my age and shy, but Marla, 12 years my senior, taught me how to read at the age of three and to count, color, and cut with a scissors. She gave me an old fashioned head start. It was a good thing for such a shy little girl to have that extra boost and I will forever be grateful to my sister. I remember sitting at the table at home when I was very young with a pad and pencil asking over and over again how to spell this word or that. Mom and Marla were always willing to answer my questions and encouraged me to write and draw.

In the mid1960s, kindergarten was a new thing in our area, and I went for half a day, five days a week. I was lucky to be assigned the afternoon session as that was what I preferred. A kindergarten bus picked me up after lunch at the end of my long driveway and I rode the big school bus on the way home with my older brothers and sister. Mrs. G. was my first teacher. She was an older, thin, and extremely tall woman. She was mean and often locked students in the classroom closet in the dark when they misbehaved. One time Mrs. G. slapped me hard across the cheek because I looked up while taking a test as she thought I was cheating. I wasn't cheating; I just had the urge to look up because she told us not to. You know how that is when someone tells you not to do something and you can't help yourself.

We didn't have desks in kindergarten. We sat in groups around little rectangular shaped children's tables with matching chairs. We had to take naps lying on mats or rugs that we brought from home and if our eyes weren't shut during the entire nap, Mrs. G. screamed at us until we pinched them shut tight with fear. She paced the floor around us watching for any open eyes like an old mother hen. It was difficult to sleep, let alone lay still on the hard floor. My school nap pad was a new rag rug my mother had bought me, not much for padding.

Thankfully my first grade teacher, Mrs. K., was very kind to me. She let me check out books from the school library which was not something first graders were allowed to do back then. She even asked me to read the books aloud to my classmates. It made me feel special and certainly boosted my self-esteem. Mrs. K. even suggested I skip a grade and go to 3rd grade after I finished 1st grade.

One of my scariest moments in first grade was riding home from school on the bus in early spring during an ice storm. The bus was sliding all over the road and could barely make it around the curve on the blacktop highway just inside our county line. I was crying from

21

fright. When we were let off the bus it was very slippery and my sibs and I crawled down our driveway to our house as we could not stand up on the thick ice that coated the ground.

Well, skipping a grade wasn't in the cards for me, and my second grade teacher was a whole different story. She particularly picked on me because I didn't like eating the school hot lunches. One time she took me to the office with me carrying my plastic tray full of food. She had high hopes that I would finish my meal while the principal watched me while I stood at the long desk in front of her. Instead, I cried for several minutes and didn't eat a bite.

We filled up a paper cone in a pink plastic holder with milk from a "milk machine" at lunch time. Often I would drink my milk up quickly and shove my mashed potatoes into the paper cup and fold the top shut hoping no one would notice. I did not like to eat vegetables, only meat, and fruit. I was teased at home about being finicky and my poor eating habits lasted for several years. My worst fear was being forced to eat potatoes or cooked peas. For some reason I couldn't hack their mushy texture.

In second grade my eyes started getting bad and my teacher sent several notes home to my parents asking them to take me to an eye doctor. My teacher kept stressing in her notes that I could not read the blackboard and she was pretty perturbed about it. Eventually Dad did take me to the nearest optometrist, Dr. J. W. Foster, in Neillsville and he told my parents I was nearsighted. I got to pick out my first pairs of glasses, first of many, and I could see clearly again. I'm sure my second grade teacher could sense my family's poverty by the way I dressed. I believe she took that out on me by treating me cruelly.

My self-esteem started going the way of the whippoorwill when I was paired up often with the class bully, a tall farm boy who smelled like cow manure. Whenever we had to walk down the halls at school holding hands with a partner, I was stuck with him every time. I cried and it did no good and I felt that my teacher enjoyed upsetting me. I dwell on her meanness even today because I blame her for my dislike of school, a dislike that carried through even into high school. I had to force myself to go most of the time; I dreaded school.

When third grade came, things looked up and through the remainder of my grade school days I did fairly well despite having low self-esteem and teachers were friendlier to me.

Girls had to wear dresses or skirts to school up until I was in 7th grade (1971). Then we were allowed to wear polyester pant suits or dress slacks. In 8th grade we could wear denim jeans as long as they were not blue. A pair of purple jeans I bought at the local grocery store was my favorite. In high school that all changed and it was good old blue jeans for me and the wider the bell bottoms and the more they dragged on the floor, the more I liked them. Extra-long blue jeans were something to irk my father with and I wore long bell bottom jeans, frayed at the bottoms, with my leather boots, every day at school.

I can jog my memories of high school days by reflecting on particular classes that I took when I wasn't wasting my time in study hall. Advanced math – nothing but mass confusion; Biology – I can still smell the formaldehyde when dissecting frogs; typing class – 72 wpm (words per minute) on an old manual typewriter; Journalism – I drew the covers for the school newspaper; Art class, I noticed Mr. C. had a roach clip on his key chain. He wasn't there very long; Survival Biology – my favorite class of all but I missed the end of the overnight campout at the year's close because I was sick; French – I dropped out after one week; English – the teacher told me I looked exactly like her daughter and I received A's in her class.

Our high school guidance counselor slept at his desk and rare moments when he was awake in his little office we'd catch him typing with one finger as we walked past his open doorway on the way to the girl's rest room. If he was to give us direction towards a career, I never saw it.

Tall and skinny metal lockers lined the hallways and my locker mate and I plastered ours with pictures of our favorite stars, Robert Redford, Jackson Browne, Bjorne Borge, cut outs from magazines hung with scotch tape. We had classes upstairs and classes downstairs with study hall in the cafeteria where we played polish football. Good times were the homecoming bonfires, dances, football games, and wrestling matches.

Physical Education, or gym class, was never one of my favorites. We had to take this class for at least three years but could opt out in our senior year so I did. Phy. Ed. brings back to my mind: gymnastics, track, volleyball, basketball, dance lessons, showers, and exercise chants like "Fingers, knuckles, palms, toes," or "We must, we must, we must build our bust". I didn't know how to use my can of deodorant after showering so I sprayed it over top of my clothes aiming it at my armpits and my classmates laughed at me.

Bell bottoms, hip huggers, big leather belts, smock tops that looked like maternity tops, clingy sweaters, these were some of the styles we wore to school every day in the 70s.

Most of my high school memories are of good times with my girlfriends. We helped each other grow up together. My school friends were the family I lacked at home.

SICKNESS

Before I was seven I had several of those pesky childhood illnesses that thankfully aren't experienced by most North American kids these days. I don't ever remember getting any vaccinations but one time a school nurse popped a sugar cube down my throat for what I thought was polio. Chicken pox was one of those epidemics you couldn't escape from but I don't remember having it. I do remember having mumps and it was miserable. I missed first grade for about two weeks with that one. My cheeks or lower sides of my face were so swollen and it hurt like heck to swallow anything. Some kind soul came to visit us and brought Oreo cookies and I was so excited. I wanted to eat one of those cookies in the worst way but took one bite and couldn't swallow so I cried instead. Measles was another one that I don't really remember having but everyone did sooner or later, me included.

Another ailment that set me back was having several earaches while I was in grade school. I don't know what caused them but they were very painful. One time I had an earache for 3 days and nights straight. When I complained, my mother told me to go lie down and put a hot washcloth over my ear.

My family never went to the doctor unless we broke a bone or were bleeding to death. I don't think I ever went to a doctor as a child but once as a teen when I had pink eye. There was a doctor for many years that had an office in the back of a drug store in the little town where I went to school. He gave me a prescription for eye drops that helped a great deal. I missed a few days of school because my eyes were quite sensitive to the bright lights then and maybe he told me I should because I was contagious.

This is not a pleasant admission but I do remember having pinworms when I was quite young. They probably came from me playing in the dirt where my brother's hound dogs pooped. When you have pin worms the main symptom is an itchy butt, and that is exactly what troubled me. Mom's remedy for that was telling me to go put some baby powder on my butt. I don't remember ever taking any medicine for worms by mouth. Luckily I didn't get the other embarrassing problem of head lice and I didn't know anyone at school that had them. They never talked about it if they did.

When I was about 12, I started having severe toothaches in my back molars. My cheeks would swell up like a chipmunk and the pain was horrible. Dad reluctantly took me to a dentist in Neillsville who pulled all four of my molars but not before giving me meds first to clear up the infection. I remember coming home with wads of gauze packed into the holes in my jaws and lying down on the bed feeling like I might die. Luckily everything healed up well and when my wisdom teeth came in I had room for all of them and still have them today.

The dentist gave my father heck for the rough shape he found my teeth in, and Dad moaned and groaned at home about my dental bills. As I child I don't remember owning or using a toothbrush. No one bought me a toothbrush and no one ever suggested the use of one. I didn't know any better.

COLD TIMES

Wisconsin winters can get pretty chilly, sometimes double digits below zero. We had a cast iron Monarch wood cook stove in the kitchen (the manufacturer was the Malleable Iron Range Company from Beaver Dam, Wisc.) and later we had a fuel oil burner for heat. There was also a wood stove in the "living room" that was oval shaped, black and made of thin metal. When the stove had a good fire roaring in it the metal turned red. It was a miracle no one ever burned the house down. I could honestly say I nearly froze to death in the wintertime when I was a kid.

None of the stoves gave off much heat unless you stood beside them. They were like having a bonfire outside. You warmed your front side, then turned around to warm your backside, then turned around and started over again, and they were smoky too. We wore lots of clothes in the house, many layers to keep warm, and yet we were still cold.

Sometimes, for a treat, Mom would open the wood cook stove oven door and lay newspapers on it. Then we could sit on a chair and place our feet up on the door to soak up the heat. She also took flat irons and warmed them in the oven and then wrapped them up in newspapers and placed them under the covers at the foot of our beds at night.

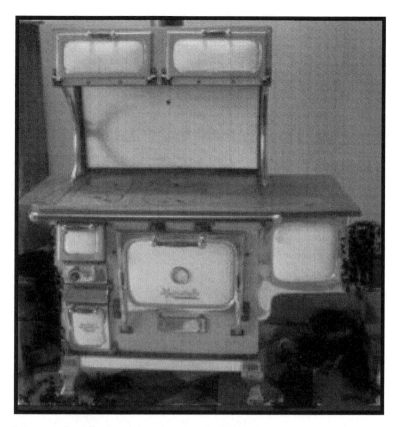

Our Monarch wood cook stove had a reservoir on the right and two warming ovens on top. There was a little ash cleanout drawer under the oven door. This isn't the stove but it looks just like it.

I don't remember my father cutting much firewood but I do remember my brothers always working at the task. They had a bucksaw and an axe and cut the wood by hand. A daily chore was to haul armloads of firewood into the house to keep the cardboard wood box filled. Dad had a Homelite chain saw that he used when cutting pulp in the woods for extra money in the winter time but I don't remember him using it much at home. My mother and I would take a cardboard box outside with a piece of twine attached to it and drag it around the edge of the woods on the snow filling it with dry broken twigs (kindling) to use for starting fires in the stoves.

Vern, Les, me, and Mom standing in front of Dad's 1962 Ford Falcon

At bedtime I'd pile several blankets on top of me to keep snug and warm. I stuck my nose out from under them so I could breathe and it was cold to the touch. I could often see my breath while in bed and dreaded getting up in the mornings to get dressed in the cold. Most winter days I changed from my flannel pajamas into my clothes underneath the covers. There was no privacy where I slept so this served two purposes; no one could see me changing clothes and I stayed warm while getting dressed.

No one bothered to fire up the stove at night anymore after Mom passed away. On the coldest days of winter when I got up in the morning for school the water buckets in the kitchen were frozen solid. The drinking dipper was frozen in a circle of ice, and mind you, this was in the 1970s. On those mornings there was no water to drink or wash up with. Going to school was alright then because I knew it would at least be warm there.

During school vacation breaks in the wintertime I'd sleep until noon, especially when I was in high school because it was warmer that way.

When someone slept half the day like me, Dad would always say, "I think you got your days and nights mixed up."

SISTER & BROTHERS

I'm six years old, and I'm tucked in for the night so I can be up and ready for school the next morning. In the room next to me, separated by a cardboard wall, my brothers sit around the kitchen table with the soft glow of the kerosene lamp burning. Their chatter makes me feel safe. They finish their homework while Mom bakes a chocolate cake in the wood cook stove oven. I can't fall asleep because I can smell it and when I hear them chowing down I ask for a piece. Mom brings me cake in a dish with a spoon. She tells me to pull the covers up tight so I won't get any crumbs in my sheets while I eat it. When everyone else goes to bed the soft glow of the kerosene lamp on the table keeps flickering... all night long, every night... I am never in the dark. That's a good thing because I'm afraid of the dark; when it's dark I feel like I can't breathe.

My oldest brother was stillborn at the hospital. He was a full term baby but died at birth when his umbilical cord wrapped around his neck and strangled him. My mother said she was able to hold her first baby whom she named Dennis and he was a cute baby with red hair. She told me that Dad took his little body home from the hospital. Dad dug the grave alone in the Sherwood Cemetery and buried his first born son in a suitcase next to his brother, Cecil's new grave. This was in the fall of 1946, seven months after Uncle Cecil passed. I think other fathers did the same thing in that time frame when there was no money for a proper burial and no one thought different of it. They had no money and took care of their own, not unlike burying a family pet in the back yard, but of course the loss of a child was much sadder.

I was lucky to have a large family. Up through first grade my sister, Marla, was always there for me. She helped take care of me and taught me so many things. I vaguely remember her being on the school bus with me as she was a senior the year I started kindergarten. It was a comfort to have a big sister riding along in the back of the bus. She graduated from school and left home in 1965 and that was a sad time for my mother and me. I don't remember seeing her too much when I was real young except for holidays like Christmas and 4th of July because it was always hard for her to get home with work and family of her own. A distance of a four hour drive seemed great back then. We wrote letters often and always kept in touch. My mother lived for those holidays when the family could be together.

My four brothers, sister, and I filled our little house up to the brim. For about five years we all lived under the same roof until one by one, my siblings moved out, and on with their lives.

L to R back row: Marla, Kent, Lynn. L to R middle row: Les, Vern.
Front row: Me. This photo was taken in about 1964. Our landmark
white pine tree stands tall and proud in the background to the right.

I don't remember my two oldest brothers, Kent and Lynn, being at home much when I was young. My two younger brothers, Vern and Les, were the ones I grew up with. They were always busy cutting firewood and hauling it in the house for Mom. They were interested in body building when in high school so used to do lots of exercises like chin-ups and push-ups and drink shakes made of raw eggs and peanut butter. Being tough was important. They read the ads in comic books featuring Arnold Schwarzenegger, the man of iron, before he became a movie star and a governor. My brothers were very hard workers, all of them. If they wanted something they had to earn money to pay for it on their own.

In the wintertime they worked at logging, cutting pulpwood, with our father. I have vivid memories of my brother, Lynn, coming home from working with Dad in the woods one day after slicing his foot open with an axe. One slip and he was a mess. He wore a cast on his leg for quite some time after that accident. My brothers also worked in moss marshes in the summer near City Point pulling and bailing sphagnum moss. That job was miserable as they were out in the hot sun all day amongst the deer flies and mosquitoes.

My third oldest brother, Vern, was the family gardener and landscaper at home. He enjoyed mowing the yard, planting vegetables in the garden, and fixing up the house as best he could using what little money he had to work with. He built a fence with birch posts along the driveway that looked really nice and a small shed with logs. Vern liked to plant trees and wanted a pond in the worst way so he was often out in the woods with a shovel trying to dig one here or there. He loved wildlife, feeding birds in the wintertime, fishing, and hunting. He was the brother I lost way too soon.

I was a nuisance to my youngest brother, Les. He is five years older than me but my closest brother in age. When young, I wanted to follow him everywhere that he went. Mom would force him to give me rides on his bicycle a mile down the road to our cousins' house; I would sit on the bar between the seat and the handlebars and hang on for dear life. We were always fighting and he would throw stuff at me or kick me until I'd run and hide and cry. This happened often but neither of us stopped the bickering.

31

When Les and I grew older we overcame our little differences and got along really well. As soon as Les finished high school he left home to live with friends and have independence. Our home life wasn't good, Mom was gone, and I don't blame him one bit for leaving me behind. He needed space.

My brothers had motorcycles, first small Honda's, and it seemed they were tinkering with them all the time and enjoyed riding them. They had at least one snowmobile, a Scorpion. It was fun to sit on the seat behind one of my brothers and ride along with brush often snapping me in the face while we blazed through the woods. When the boys started driving, Les bought a green Chevy Carry-All van. It was fun to ride with him and listen to 8-track tapes playing on his rigged up tape player, the louder the music the better. Foghat and Led Zepplin were some of his favorites.

Les and Vern with their motorcycles at home, about 1970

My oldest brother, Kent, was married not long after he finished high school to a neighbor girl in 1970. Kent and Lynn took jobs working

32

with our Dad on road construction. They did cement work building sidewalks, curbs, and gutters in many cities throughout Wisconsin. Both of them were drafted during the Vietnam War. Lynn entered the Army and was sent to the DM Zone between North and South Korea. Kent was in the hospital with a concussion at about the time his draft letter came. He'd been playing baseball for a team in a neighboring township and was struck on the side of his head by a pitched ball. The injury left him unconscious, blood running from his ears. He was hospitalized for ten days and his doctor did not recommend him being drafted.

Kent with his buck, Grandpa's log shed and grinding wheel in the background, mid 1960s. This same oak tree is also in the next photo.

It was hard on Mom seeing Lynn go into the service. Mom, Marla and I wrote letters to him often. I remember one day when we got the mail there was another letter from the draft board and Mom began crying as soon as she read the return address. She knew what it was, another draft letter for Vern. After basic training with the Army, Vern was stationed in Germany, a safe place I guess, but not a happy place for him. I'm sure the time Lynn and Vern spent in the service was a reminder to Mom of all those years she waited for our dad to be discharged from the Army during World War II.

Lynn, with one of his first recurve bow-killed deer, at home, early 1960s. In the background is Grandpa's outhouse to the left of the tree. The log shed is behind Lynn.

LUXURIES OF HOME

I'm four years old. It's cold outside tonight, just right for making Jello. Mom heats up some water in the teakettle on the cook stove, measures it out, pours it into a bowl, and stirs in a large box of strawberry flavored gelatin powder with a wooden spoon. Then she adds the cold water to it and sits the bowl outside until it sets. It won't be long until we can all enjoy some strawberry Jello.

Vern and Les at the kitchen table with our best kerosene reading lamp, an Aladdin. I see at least four calendars on the wall. We tacked up every free one we collected from local places of business. My favorite calendars had a pocket and a pencil with them.

My sister and older brothers spent most or all of their days in the 1950s and early '60s growing up without ever having electricity in our home and had to face living with this stigma all through school. When my sister's first boyfriend walked her home one evening from roller skating at the town hall down the road she didn't want him to see the kerosene lamp burning in the window. Being the youngest of the family, I was lucky enough to have the luxury of electricity, crude as it was, not long after I started grade school.

I'll try to paint a picture of the kitchen in our little home. The kitchen was sometimes the warmest room in the house when Mom was baking. There was always a teakettle with warm water sizzling on the cook stove. We washed dishes on the stove in a large enamel dish pan while another dishpan filled with hot water was used to rinse off the dishes. Mom had a 1940s "Hoosier" style cupboard with a flour sifter bin on the top left and shelves to store sugar, spices, etc. in. In the bottom half of the cupboard was a silverware drawer and other drawers for dishtowels, and a door that opened with shelves to store canned goods.

Next to the kitchen cupboard was a table with an enamel wash pan and two white enamel water buckets with an enamel dipper in one of them. A mirror hung on the wall above the water buckets. I can't fail to mention the way we pitched out our wash-up water and table scraps. Under the water bucket table we had what we called a slop pail. It was just a plastic bucket that sat there until it was filled up to the brim waiting for someone to lug it out behind the house and dump it. The contents of the bucket gave off an unpleasant odor usually. It was never scrubbed out so you can imagine how nasty it was. Thing of it was, we never gave having a slop bucket a second thought. It was just part of our way of living.

The kitchen table was in the middle of the room with wooden chairs around it where we all sat to eat and do our school homework, etc. A red and white checkered plastic tablecloth with flannel backing covered the table and was replaced with a new one once a year.

On the opposite wall was a metal cupboard with doors and shelves inside where we stored our dishes. Later a refrigerator stood next to the metal cupboard. Dad always sat at the head of the table where an ashtray was handy as well as his coffee cup. Next to Dad's chair, against the wall, were an old stuffed chair, an old overstuffed sofa (the one the rat died in) and Grandma's sewing machine. Next to the wood cook stove was a cardboard box that we threw firewood in, a kerosene stove for cooking, and later, a fuel oil burner for heat.

We had our house electrified very simply back in 1965 or 1966. My father was away working at his road construction job (he was a cement finisher, mainly doing the finishing touches on sidewalks and curb and gutter) when my mother found the name of a man who did electrical work. I believe he had the reputation of being "reasonable". She hired him to come to the house and wire it up while Dad was away at work. This electrician, who seemed quiet elderly to me, put a 15 amp fuse box on the wall in the kitchen. There were little glass fuses that you had to screw out and replace in the box when they "blew". Luckily the fuses were cheap because they blew often. The electrician installed a few wall outlets and a few sockets into the ceiling to screw light bulbs into. My brother recalled how he broke a hole in the roof above the bedroom when he climbed up there for some reason. The poor man must have stepped on a weak spot. When Dad came home from work at the end of that week he was hopping mad. I suppose he didn't know how he'd manage to pay the electric bill each month. But he did and I think he accepted it and liked it later on.

Our neighbor, Gladys, brought my mother a toaster, which I embraced by stuffing it with Pop-tarts. Mom bought an electric fry pan that she could adjust the temperature on and a deep fat fryer for cooking chicken. She filled the fryer up with lard and used the same lard over and over. Mom also bought a two burner hotplate and it was very useful for frying up eggs or heating up a pan of soup or just about anything. She'd been living almost twenty years with no electricity when nearly every neighbor in the community already had that luxury for years.

After we got the electricity hooked up, Mom still used the oven in the wood cook stove for baking in cool weather. On Sundays she would fill up a large black enamel roaster with chicken and vegetables, or a beef roast, and we'd head off to church. When we came home it would be ready, a real treat. She also baked the most delicious cinnamon rolls in the cook stove oven. Often she'd be popping them out about the time we came home from school in the winter.

We acquired a used refrigerator from somewhere and that was probably the best part of having electricity, that and having brighter lighting at night. Having a frig meant that we could have ice cream in the little freezer compartment at the top of it. And we could have cold milk and a variety of meats... and we could make Jello anytime of the year!

Prior to this, all her married life, Mom had to store cold items in a hole behind the house dug in the ground about three feet deep. I remember the hole had a lid made of lumber thrown over top of it to keep the rain and the critters out. Food did not keep very long in the hole, especially meat. When we did buy meat or had venison processed, we stored the bulk of it at the locker plant in Pittsville. We paid a rental fee to store meat there, and brought home a few packages on our weekly trips to town for groceries. Keeping meat at home in winter wasn't such a problem, but at other times of the year it had to be used up quickly.

For a short time we also had a kerosene stove for cooking. It was stinky and messy. We filled the burners with a big tin funnel and it spilled easily.

I remember when Dad brought home a small black and white portable TV for Mom one Friday night when he came home from work. Mom loved it but Dad seldom watched it. I think the TV cost about $145.00. It had a 14" screen and rabbit ears we sometimes wrapped with tinfoil. Mom watched every soap opera she could find each week day. Television was one of her few enjoyments in life and she had a lot of catching up to do. Some of the shows that I remember her watching were "Days of Our Lives" (Like sands through the hourglass, these are the days of our lives) and "As the World Turns". In the winter when my father was not working I noticed him watching the soap operas too sometimes when I was home from school.

In 1969, when the astronauts first landed on the moon, I begged Dad to watch the live news coverage on TV with me and he reluctantly did. It seemed after that he watched television more often.

In the winters when Dad was off work (you can't pour cement in Wisconsin in the wintertime) he spent much of his time in the kitchen sitting at the table. I can still visualize him sitting there with a cup of coffee nearby and a lit cigarette in his hand reading the newspaper. It was there sitting in his kitchen chair that he got out the checkbook and paid the bills. It was there he read his Louis L'Amour western paperbacks, Reader's Digest condensed books, the daily newspaper comic strips, and he tackled the crossword puzzles. It was there in the kitchen where he often put his head down on the table and fell asleep, cigarette still burning between his fingers.

We always had a radio in the kitchen. Before our home was electrified my mother had a white plastic radio that only brought in A.M. stations and operated with "D" size batteries. Those batteries were handy in our flashlights too. She liked the local radio station at Neillsville the best but it generally went off the air at about 5 p.m. Mom liked to listen to polkas when she could find them on the radio early on Sunday mornings. One of my favorite polka songs as a young child was, "Little Brown Jug". Another of my first favorite hit songs on the radio was "Little Boxes" by Pete Seeger. I loved music and so did Mom. More than music, I think she liked the noise the radio brought into our little house.

It was about 1969 when a telephone came into our home. I don't remember my father being upset about getting the phone connected, but I'm sure he was. He never answered it or called anyone from what I can remember; I guess he had no reason to. My mother did enjoy it though. I used our phone mostly to talk with my friends in evenings after school and in summertime when I seldom saw them. Ours was a tan colored phone with a rotary dial and our number was imprinted in a circle in the center of the dial. We rented it from the phone company for a monthly fee that showed up on our bill along with the calling fees. There was a huge difference in the cost of calls from daytime versus nighttime. If you waited until after 9 p.m. you got a much better deal. If you called during business hours on week days they really whopped you. Weekend rates were also cheaper than week day rates by far.

We had a "party line" that we shared with about six other neighbors who lived north, west, east, and south of us. If I used the phone too much and tied up the line, the neighbors would pick up, tell me it was an emergency and that I should get off of the line immediately. I always did hang right up but I doubted the seriousness of their pleas. I could tell when someone else on our party line picked up while I was talking because I could hear a difference in the tone, especially if they picked up their receiver quickly. When a person took their phone off the hook to use it and heard someone else's conversation it was tempting to listen in, and yes, I was guilty of that myself.

Sometimes you don't miss things you never had. That was the case with me in regards to having no indoor bathroom or running water. But mind you, this was in the 1960s and 1970s when most everyone else had these conveniences. You didn't talk about the fact that you had no "facilities" with your friends at school. As far as they were concerned your house was modern and up to date and you hoped no one would find out the truth. If they did you lost a friend. It happened to me in fourth grade when I invited my best friend to come stay overnight at my house. I thought we had a good time but when we went back to school the next day she wouldn't speak to me and never really spoke to me again. I suffered pretty hard over that one, but it taught me a lesson to keep my friends away and apart from my home life.

Our only source for all of our water was Grandpa Adam's pitcher pump well when I was young. We carried two empty metal enamel water buckets up the hill to Grandpa's well in front of his cabin whenever we needed water for dishes, washing up, or drinking. At least it was downhill when we carried the full buckets back to our house. It was better to carry two to balance yourself out, than just one full bucket. An enamel drinking ladle or dipper bobbed around in one of the buckets and we all used it to sip water from or to fill up a glass. The universal dipper was white with red trim around the cup and the handle.

We heated water in teakettles on the cook stove to wash up with or do dishes with. We used a big metal enamel pan for dish wash water and a smaller enamel pan for "washing up" with a wash cloth. After electricity came, we could heat water up on a hot plate for dishes, etc. Most of the time there was no privacy, and the house was way too cold to wash up, so we didn't bother. After a while we'd get what old timer's called "winter bark" on our skin. It was kind of like having a sun tan, but blotchy. When I think of it now it seems extremely gross. When spring came, and it was warm enough to go swimming again at the lake down the road, it was a welcome chance to scrub our "winter bark" off.

The outhouse was out back of our house down a well-worn path through the woods. It was all we ever had in my growing up years. It was cold in the winter and smelly in the summer. Everyone used it and they had to keep digging new holes and moving it around when the hole filled up. We didn't think much of it. We had a couple white enamel pots to pee in when it was very cold out or at night, one downstairs and one upstairs for my brothers. One time my brothers tipped over their full pee pot while horsing around upstairs and pee ran down the woodstove pipe. The pipe was hot with a fire going in the stove and the smell of the sizzling pee running down it was awful.

When I was a teenager, or maybe a little younger, Dad decided to dig a new well and for some reason we stopped using Grandpa's. The new well was a little closer to our house and between the circle part of our driveway. It was dug to a depth of 15 feet and Dad placed a sand point in the hole.

My dad liked to witch for water so I'm sure that is why he picked that spot for the new well. He would take his jack knife and cut a live green twig with a fork in it shaped like a "Y" for a witching tool. Then he'd place the fork of the twig between the palms of his upturned hands and let the tip of the twig stick out parallel to the ground. He'd slowly walk along waiting for the stick to point down to the ground. It would neatly slip through his palms and turn straight downward when he found water. Watching that forked stick turn down at the same place again and again after pacing back and forth was a sure sign this was the spot to dig, a good source of water.

Our new well did give us plenty of water but it wasn't as nice as Grandpa's well. We had to prime the pitcher pump attached to the sand point before any water would come up. That meant carrying water out to the well, pouring it down the pump, and pumping on the handle like crazy until the water started to come up into it. In the winter time we had to heat the water that we used to prime the pump and if it didn't work we'd have to go back to the house and get more heated up water and try it again. I'm sure it was just surface water we were bringing up with that shallow well but we never got sick from it. The water was very clear, soft and gentle for washing hair, etc.

Not far from the house, to the north, was a trail into the woods adorned with huge mounds of garbage along both sides of it. This was where we pitched anything we couldn't burn such as tin cans, bottles, broken dishes, light bulbs, car license plates, flash light batteries, etc. The further away from the house you walked the older the piles were, as time passed we got lazier and didn't carry things as far. The garbage piles were far enough away that you couldn't see them from the house, out of sight, out of mind. I think that was the general idea of the outhouse too, keeping it far enough away from the house so you couldn't see it.

When my siblings were young, Mom washed clothes outside with a wringer washer that had a gas motor on it. She would have her niece come and help her get it started sometimes as Mom didn't have the strength to push her foot down hard enough on the pedal to crank it up. She hung the wash on the clothesline, a wire strung between a few wooden posts stuck in the ground. I think the washer went to heck later on because I don't remember using it at all. It sat out in the yard under a pine tree near the clothesline for many years. When I was young, my mother, father, and I went to Pittsville to do our laundry almost every Saturday. Our trip was a weekly ritual, and that's another story.

STUFF

I'm nine years old and my best friend from school, the infamous Gail, comes for a sleep-over at my house. It's the first time I've ever had a friend, not related to me, stay overnight. Gail says, "Who sleeps in that baby crib in the middle room?" I tell her we let my two year old nephew sleep in it when he comes to visit. Gail says she thinks she knows better... I cringe and say no more.

My first memories of the furnishings in the room I shared with my parents were of my bed and potty chair that had a thin sheet of red formica cut in the shape of a square to cover it. I slept in what was called a six year baby crib with railings on the sides and tall foot and head boards with decals on them. I can't remember what the decals were but it seemed like they were yellow baby ducks. I slept in this supposed six year crib well past my ninth birthday. I shudder when I think about how that baby crib was all I had to sleep in and why somebody didn't do something about it. Such apathy! Because I was the "baby" of the family, did that mean I would never grow up or did they hope I never would? In order to sleep in the crib, I had to curl up in a fetal position with my head pressed against the headboard and my knees always drawn up to my chest.

When it became apparent to little me that Grandpa Adam was not well enough to come back home to live in his cabin anymore I asked my mother if I could have his single bed. I suppose my brothers brought it down to our house from Grandpa's cabin for me. I'm guessing it was the summer I turned 10, after the "Gail" incident. It was an antique metal bed with circular bases on the legs with holes drilled in them. The entire frame was cast iron and painted dark blue. Someone said it was a bed from a Navy ship; the holes were for screws to fasten it down to the floor of the ship so that it wouldn't move around, and I think that assumption was correct. The width of the bed was quite narrow but it was plenty long and a real improvement from the six year baby crib for me.

I also asked for Grandpa's walnut three drawer dresser and put it near my new bed. Before this, all I had to store my clothes in was a large cardboard box about three feet tall and two feet wide. I can still visualize the large yellow and black truck printed on the side of that cardboard box advertising a moving company. Mainly I filled my box with socks, underwear, pants, and t-shirts. My dresses, for school and church, were hung on hangers by my mother's dresses so they weren't wrinkled like my other clothes.

I liked to take an ink pen and doodle on the wall above my bed in the evenings when I couldn't sleep and everyone else was still up in the room next to me. It was easy to hang pictures on the cardboard walls with a thumbtack. Mom had embroidered two cloth pictures that her father made wooden frames for before she was married. One hung above her bed with two colorful parrots on it and the other hung on the wall in the hallway and was of "The Lord's Prayer". Both of the frames were covered with glass. I still have the parrots and my sister has the prayer picture.

I can't remember having any furniture other than Grandpa's bed and walnut dresser that I could call my own. I had a big cardboard shoebox that I stored all my little treasures in. I liked to collect little toys such as Cracker Jack prizes and trinkets from penny bubble gum machines and had quite an assortment of them. I was a little hoarder, and I'm still a hoarder. To this day I have a weakness for items to store things in such as wooden boxes of all sizes and wooden cupboards with shelves in them. I think it's because when I was young I never had a decent place to store my things.

SATURDAYS

I'm eight years old, it's Saturday, and Mom and I are unloading our wooden bushel baskets filled with dirty clothes and powdered laundry soap from the trunk of the car and carrying them into the laundromat. We don't have enough quarters so we walk down to the bank and get the change we need for the machines. My aunt, uncle, and cousins show up to do their laundry as well. Once we get the wash loaded in the machines I ask Mom if I can walk to the drugstore with my cousins to buy some gum. We save the gum wrappers sometimes for making paper chains.

Leaving the country and going to town on Saturdays was something we looked forward to and dreaded at the same time. Mom never learned to drive and with Dad working, that was our day. All in all it was nice to go to town, do a little shopping, and visit with my cousins if they happened to be there doing laundry and getting groceries too.

I remember the sulfur smell of the gas dryers, the heat they gave off in the summer time, and a few of the same people who we chatted with there each time. My mother made friends with some of the women so it was a social event for her as well. In the summer the laundromat was so hot. I helped Mom add soap to the washers, put the money in the machines, and fold the clothes after taking them out of the dryers. We used about five or six washing machines. The machines took two or three quarters and the dryers ran on dimes. Sometimes you'd get a dryer that was a dud, waste a couple dimes in it, and then have to transfer the still wet load to a different dryer. It took a long time to finish the task, especially if the place was crowded and you had to wait your turn to use the machines.

After we finished our laundry we shopped at Ray's One Stop for our next week's supply of groceries. Sometimes we went to the meat locker down the street to pick up a few packages of frozen venison stored there. The locker plant sold great tasting roasts, freshly made sausage, and hamburger. It smelled good in there too. One of our favorite treats was fresh beef liver. Mom would roll it in flour and fry it with onions not long after we came home from town.

If my cousins were in town too, we often walked down the sidewalk together to the drug store carefully looking over the new comic books and ice cream treats. Mom would shop at the drug store if she needed greeting cards or something special, like Polident to clean her and Dad's false teeth. My parents both got their first sets of false teeth when they were in their late thirties or early forties.

The dreaded part of our trip to town came when our chores were all done. Mom and I had to put on our walking shoes and figure out which tavern Dad had his butt parked in. There were at least five taverns within walking distance from the grocery store and laundromat that he could choose from. His favorite hangouts were "Boney's Bar" and "The Wagon Wheel". It was a major chore getting him to leave once we found him. He was usually well on the way to being quite drunk by the time we left town and headed for home.

After we bought our supply of groceries for another week and got our clean clothes all loaded up in the car, with Dad at the wheel, we headed for home and held our breath tightly. There was another tavern called "The Hill Top" on a little hill just a mile out of town, and if Dad was in a certain mood our Ford would find its way into that "Hill Top" parking lot, sure enough. There was nothing to do but go inside and join him while he slugged down a few more beers. Then we'd start nagging again for him to shake a leg. On a good Saturday, he'd just breeze on by that little bar on the hill and head for home as Mom and I breathed a sigh of relief.

My mother was sick with cancer and in the hospital so often after I turned 11. I did the laundry and grocery shopping myself while Dad waited in one of the taverns as usual. When I got everything done I'd walk up and down the sidewalks on main street to each tavern and stand on my tip toes, peering into the windows to see which one he was in. It was really embarrassing to walk in the door and stare at all the people sitting on the bar stools and then have to walk back out if he wasn't there.

"Ray's One Stop" allowed me to charge the groceries that I picked out and loaded into our car when I was shopping alone. When Dad was ready to go home he would go in the store with me and pay the bill. He was often quite drunk by then, struggling with his wallet, and full of smiles. I wondered what the lady that owned the store thought of him. Probably not much I suppose, because it was like that almost every weekend. I learned many years later that her husband was an alcoholic himself.

Once in a great while my mother and I had a chance to go shopping in other towns besides Pittsville. When my dad had to sign up for unemployment in late fall in Wisconsin Rapids we went to Johnson Hills, a huge department store with clothing. Dad found a tavern downtown that was within walking distance of this store so we knew where to find him when we were done.

A few times each year we went to Neillsville. My favorite store there was the dime store. It was huge and had lots of toys, candy, and knickknacks to choose from. Once in a great while we went to the shoe store. As soon as you walked in the door you could smell leather from all the open boxes of shoes. The owner helped you find the kind of shoes you were looking for and carried a stool around with him for you to sit on. You'd put your foot up on it while he sat at the other end of it. He would put the shoes on your feet, tighten up the laces properly, and let you walk around the store in them. He had a measuring tool he used to check the width and length of your feet. Shoe shopping was rare but wonderful. My mother loved shoes.

Near or above the shoe store in Neillsville on a second floor was a chiropractor's office where my grandfather went when he was still able to climb the stairs. There were also two laundromats to choose from in Neillsville. Dad liked to go to a tavern near the shoe store called "Snowball's Bar" at that time. The drugstore in town had some good deals too and we usually went to a large store across from the library called the Farmer's Store. There you could find everything;

47

clothing, hardware, and furniture. It was as close as you could get to a Walmart atmosphere today.

MY FATHER'S VICES

I'm 10 and in the wee hours of the morning I awaken on this cold winter day to a room filled with smoke. Mom is rushing around our little house trying to awaken my two older brothers who are fast asleep upstairs. I'm coughing from the smoke, but my dad doesn't wake up and he is sleeping in the same room as me. My brothers come to Mom's rescue. They trudge down the stairs to find the stuffed chair in the kitchen on fire. They carry the heavy chair out the door and whoosh the smoke out the door as best they can. We all try to go back to sleep. When we leave the house that morning and walk up the driveway to wait for the school bus, I see our stuffed chair still smoldering in the yard. Dad had dropped a lit cigarette in the chair and went to bed. He was still sleeping when we left for school. Maybe a lot of kids were going through the same things that I was, I wasn't really sure.

Dad always had a lit cigarette burning in his right hand between his stained yellow fingers. Regular Camels were his favorite. He often rolled his own smokes in the wintertime with Top and later Bugler Tobacco and used Zig Zag papers. I can easily picture him sleeping at the kitchen table with a lit cigarette in his hand, ashes falling onto the table, his lap, or the floor, and a full ashtray nearby. His every day work shirts and pants were dotted with little cigarette burns and so was the upholstery in his car. I think the smoking habit for Dad was probably set in his Army days during World War II, when soldiers were given free cigarettes with their rations.

48

As mentioned, Saturday's trip to town usually ended with Dad driving home drunk in the middle of the day. Getting from Pittsville to our house was often a chore. When it was just he and I in the car I'd make sure Dad stayed awake and I also tried to help him stay on his side of the road.

In a vivid memory of mine on an early Saturday afternoon Dad is struggling with a match trying to light a cigarette and is getting frustrated. I plead with him, "Dad, let me light up your cigarette for you," as I grab his book of matches, rip one out, and strike it. I put the lit match on the end of his cigarette which is embedded in the right side of his mouth and I'm successful. His cigarette lights up and he is good to go as we continue down the highway. I keep a steady chatter in hopes he will stay awake until we get to our driveway about 10 miles further down the road.

Dad smoked several packs of cigarettes daily, bought or home rolled. Our house was always smoky in the wintertime when it was shut up. You could see a continual blue haze in the air. If one wasn't lit between Dad's fingers, a cigarette was idly burning in the ashtray. The smoking continued until he started coughing up blood, a sign of emphysema. After a doctor told him he had to quit, he succeeded, but then switched to chewing Copenhagen tobacco.

The Saturday daytime tavern visit in town was never enough for Dad. He would end up driving up to the local tavern just around the corner almost every Saturday night and then repeat this again on Sunday afternoon or evening. Dad's drinking was another reason that I was embarrassed to have any of my friends come to our house or meet him, one big factor contributing to my low-self-esteem. He would sometimes take a two day break from drinking in the wintertime, but then he'd always go right back to the alcohol.

One thing Dad never failed to do though was get up and drive to work on Monday mornings. I don't ever remember him missing work because he'd been drinking and for this I am thankful. Dad always paid the bills on time, and even with all the drinking he still managed to save a reserve in the bank. I never saw him appear to have a hangover, complain about a headache, or throw up from drinking too much. Perhaps he felt sick sometimes, but he never complained. And he always kept a neat appearance, wore clean clothes, polished his shoes, and wore a nice hat. It was like he lived two different lives sometimes... the hard worker and provider for his family... and the drunk at the tavern night after night. When I think about that now, it was pretty amazing how he could pull it off year after year, living the lifestyle he did.

Dad, cigarette in his right hand, and me, with one of my brother's hound dogs

ROCKS

Dad was a rock lover and I am too. He would walk the garden, the driveway, anywhere he could eye the bare ground to look for small rocks. His favorites were Lake Superior agates and tiny, polished and solid colored smooth pebbles. He'd carry them around in his pockets and put them in jars. I'm sure Dad learned this from his father.

Grandpa Adam had a "rock table" in the yard under an oak tree where he placed his favorite rocks. I would stand there as a young child and look at his rock collection, time and again, finding fascination in the odd shapes, textures, and colors. One particular rock was red, shaped like a foot, and it was life sized. Grandpa wondered if Native Americans may have used the rock as a mold for sewing moccasins. Other rocks from Grandpa's collection that I liked were those with bits of mica in them that twinkled in the sunlight. There were beautiful rocks of all shapes and kinds on Grandpa's rock table.

Grandpa would put his favorite smaller rocks in jars filled with water and store them in his cabin. He said that rocks always looked prettier when they were wet and he was right!

Once Dad took a piece of light purple colored quartz, or maybe it was glass, and chipped it into a tiny arrowhead. He would have been great at flint knapping.

When I was quite young Dad took me arrowhead hunting. After one time, I was hooked for life. We would walk a freshly plowed field in the springtime, just after a heavy rainfall. We never found more than one or two arrowheads but many bits or pieces from the making of them, that we called chips. I learned to focus on certain colors of rock

51

as I walked along, light colored quartz that twinkled in the sunlight, or off white or gray colored stones called chert. In addition to the color of the stones, I learned to focus on the thickness of them, as arrowheads are always thin on the edges. Arrowhead hunting was a springtime ritual that I really looked forward to, but we didn't go often enough.

To this day I love collecting interesting rocks, fossils, arrowheads, and especially Lake Superior agates. I consider the appreciation of rocks a wonderful gift from my grandpa and my dad.

DRUNK DRIVING

I'm 14 and I'm riding with Dad in his car. He's driving me home in the middle of the night from Sherwood Park where some of his friends were camping out and having a beer party. We're a mile down the road from the campgrounds when a cop begins to follow us and turns on his flashers. Dad pulls over; the cop comes up to his window and asks him to exit the car. He tells my dad to walk the centerline and shines a flashlight on the dotted line in the middle of the road but Dad doesn't do so well. Then the cop asks him to touch his nose with his finger, that doesn't fair well either. Dad is read his rights and arrested for drunk driving.

They didn't call it an OWI back then and they didn't have breathalyzer tests. They sniffed your breath with their schnoz and if they smelled booze they made you walk the dotted centerline of the highway, if there was one. Dad and I had to get into the police car and he was handcuffed. I begged the cop to drop me off at home just three miles down the road, not far off the route to the county jail. He agreed, and took me home. It was about 3:00 a.m. I couldn't sleep too good the rest of the night wondering how Dad was going to fair on this one and how he was going to get home the next day.

When Dad was taken to the county jail that night, the officers threw his car keys on the floor and told him to pick them up. He told me that he said, "You threw them keys on the floor, you pick them dam keys up." Dad got out of that one after hiring an attorney named Hughie Haight, dubbed by the news media back in the day as Neillsville's colorful lawyer, and his fine was whittled down to "deviating to the left of center". I can't remember how many times Dad did actually lose his license to drunk driving. It happened quite a bit.

Dad's loss of a license was a real hardship on my mother who never learned to drive a car. She had to bum rides with relatives and neighbors when she needed to get to town. There was the embarrassment of it all, hoping everyone didn't find out, including Mom's own family. We wondered what the neighbors were saying.

Dad preferred Pabst Blue Ribbon, on tap, in a 7 oz. Pabst Blue Ribbon glass. Occasionally he'd ask for a raw egg in his beer glass. He would get a chuckle or two from bystanders when he'd down the beer and egg without gagging. Sometimes he'd ask for a shot glass of whiskey to go along with the beer. Dad liked to drink his beer in taverns. He never drank beer at home.

Every little town nearby had a favorite hangout. The closest town had five of those little gems on main street. Taverns were smoky affairs, with their usual drunks sitting on their usual barstools. Sometimes the individual bartender was the reason Dad chose where he liked to drink; perhaps a good looking woman, or a man who had a gift of gab. And there were taverns along the way between the little towns as well. Our Fords knew every one of them, and veered into all of their parking lots, sucking themselves in like a magnet.

The only thing I liked about taverns when I was a kid was the fact that they baked darn good pizzas, sold candy bars, had pinball machines, and dime shakes in which you could win a prize. You'd give the bartender a dime for a chance to shake the dice and try to get the highest numbers, such as six dice each with six up. My most memorable prizes from winning those dime shakes were a gold glass piggybank full of dimes and a very nice hatchet in a leather sheath.

For the most part, I detested our Ford's magnetism to taverns. We spent a lot of wasted time in them, did a lot of nagging and begging to go home, a lot of "please, please, please can we go now", and we always worried if we'd make it home safely every time we ended up in one. "We" was my mother and I. There was one good thing about my dad... the drunker he got the slower he drove... so if a ditch was in his future, he slowly drove into it, and fell asleep at the wheel afterward.

When I was 15, I passed my learner's permit at school, so I could officially drive with a licensed adult accompanying me in the car. One night after midnight I was with Dad at a tavern and he was so plowed he could barely walk. We were ten miles from home and although I'd never driven before, I thought this was the time, so I volunteered to drive his Ford Maverick and he actually said o.k. We made our way to the car and after I put it in reverse, we heard a big bang. I had backed into a truck parked next to us. I got out and looked over the situation in the dark as best I could, saw no damage, and away we went. I didn't know how to steer a car; I'd never driven a tractor or anything like it before. I kept swerving back and forth across the centerline, over correcting my steering. Dad said I drove "weird", but at least we made it home.

Dad's 1973 Ford Maverick. He bought it brand new.

TURMOIL

I'm seven and Mom and I get up in the morning and look out the window through the sagging front door of our home. We see a car parked in the yard, but it's not our car. It's white, our car is white, but it's not our white Ford Falcon. It's a Chevy of some sort. Dad is sleeping off a drunk and we're not going to wake him. Later a neighbor, who I think knows more than we know, calls to say another neighbor had his white car stolen from the Hilltop Bar down the road, the night before. That neighbor's car sits in our yard... it wasn't stolen. It's just the same color, that's all.

My parents were always fighting. Mainly it was Dad, drunk, hollering at Mom. He made her cry almost every day he was with her. He drug her down, called her stupid, hollered about her spending money on shoes, purses, and coats. I never saw him hit her, but the verbal abuse was loud and harsh and Mom took it all in. She never threatened to leave Dad. I wondered in my child's mind how she could take all that abuse, why she didn't divorce him. I wanted her to divorce him and in fact I begged her to divorce him when I was a little girl... but she never did. She loved him, simple as that.

When Dad would come home on a Friday night, after being away all week on his road construction job, he would eat supper, clean up, and drive up to the local bar. Sometimes he didn't get home from work until late and was already drunk and angry, especially if Mom didn't have a hot meal ready for him. She tried, but it was hard with just the wood stove and the hot plate for cooking, and the uncertainty of when he would get home.

I often wonder if my mother was not my father's choice for marriage. Although they dated for ten years, for several of them he was away in C.C.C. camps and he spent five years in the Army during WWII. When he was finally released from service my mother had their wedding all planned to take place just a month after he came home in September of 1945. She did not want to wait any longer for him. I suppose he didn't really see a way out. But I'd say she was the best thing that could have happened to him and I hope he realized it.

At first my parents lived with my mother's mother (Grandma in Iowa) as her father had just passed away. Then that winter my father's brother, Cecil, died when he ran his car into a snow filled road ditch. The car was stuck so he slept in it and left it running to keep warm on that cold January night. The tail pipe was packed shut with snow and the exhaust backed up into the car and got the best of him. My uncle had survived the horrors of war, a paratrooper with the 101st Airborne, and only had a few months back home in Wisconsin before he left this world. My grandfather was very lonely after losing his favorite son so he asked my newlywed parents to move in with him. And that is what they did in 1946.

Mom and Dad made their makeshift home that next summer in what was the supposed to be Uncle Cecil's garage, just west of Grandpa's log cabin home. They shared the same yard and driveway. My grandfather had previously written a will leaving his 80 acres to Cecil.

56

It took Grandpa another 25 years to put the deed in my father's name even though Mom and Dad lived there continuously the whole time. Needless to say, they didn't get along that well, Dad and Grandpa. One sore spot was Dad's drinking. I'm not sure what the rest of the trouble was but I think their personalities clashed. My mom never knew if her home was ever going to be her and Dad's place "on paper". It was always a worry for her with no sense of security.

The trauma from Dad's war memories, peer pressure, depression, and poverty probably enforced his drinking habits. I didn't notice any shaky hands when he didn't have a drink for a long time so perhaps he wasn't a true alcoholic. One of his expressions that he said often, with a bitter tone was, "You're just a victim of circumstances, just a damn victim of circumstances." I felt that he meant it, at least to some extent, in regards to who one ends up with as a life partner. And then again I think he meant it literally and here I'll share with you one of the two stories he told me about being in the war.

Dad said one day one of his Army buddies refused to get into his foxhole for protection when the enemy's heavy shelling was threatening. The reason he refused was because he noticed a scorpion in the foxhole. Shortly afterward a shell landed directly in that foxhole so that fear of the scorpion saved his buddy's life. But then again, one thing led to another, his buddy was just a lucky victim of circumstance.

*Dad in the middle, with his Army buddies in a bunker
during World War II, over there somewhere.*

Dad & Mom about 1939, in Iowa. They dated for ten years before getting married. Mom never gave up on him and loved him unconditionally.

CHURCH

Sunday mornings in my young world always included church services. My mother and I put on our best dresses and walked side by side to the little Lutheran Church adjacent to our driveway out by the highway. Rev. E. T. Keller was pastor for many years and we liked him. He was friendly to everyone and didn't show any partiality.

Mom brought along her church envelope filled with money to put in the collection dish when it was passed. The envelopes were furnished by the church; all confirmed members were given a year's supply of them in late December or early January with their names stamped on the front. At the end of each year a report (several copied pages) was given to all the households of church members that tallied up how much each person had donated for the year. It didn't look good if there was a very small amount (or no total) behind someone's name so Mom made sure all of her confirmed kids had money for their envelopes too. My family's annual tithing total wasn't much, but it was something for the record.

Mom made sure we had nice clothes for church, especially for Easter. Sometimes we would order dresses and purses and shoes from the Montgomery Ward catalogue (she called it Monkey Wards). Mom also ordered fake fur coats from the mail order company called Fingerhut, also hats, shoes, and everything from sheets to towels. A favorite dress I remember wearing to church in springtime was made of light green crepe material with a belt. It was such a pretty dress, one that I felt excited to wear to both church and school for the short time it fit me.

St. Paul's Lutheran Church at Sherwood as it looks today

Mom and I dressed up for Sunday church in 1967

Church was comforting in its own way and left me with a warm and fuzzy feeling. We always sat in the same church pew on the right side of the church toward the back, next to Glenn and Doris. Everyone at church always sat in the same pews, like cows going to their stalls. Doris was Mom's friend who also died of cancer. Doris sang loud, and deeply, and she had beautiful red hair and lots of freckles. My mother sang all the hymns too and I tried to follow along by reading the lyrics out of the blue hymnal books that were neatly tucked in wooden holders behind each pew.

Each Sunday, before church service, our congregation held Sunday School classes in the little musty church basement and Mom made sure I went, just as all my brothers and sister had before me. There were five or six kids in each class according to what grades we were in at school. Some of the kids couldn't read very well when it was their turn to read aloud from the weekly bible lessons so they were made fun of. Thankfully, I was a good little reader. The neighbor ladies who had children in Sunday School taught classes, but my mother never did.

At Christmas time the kids put on a program for all parents and church members to attend. At our program we recited bible verses that we were asked to memorize and we acted out the nativity story in a little skit. We also sang many Christmas songs such as "Silent Night", "Noel", and "Away in a Manger". At the close of the service all the children were treated with a little brown paper bag full of hard Christmas candy, an apple, and peanuts in the shell. A candy cane stuck out of the top of the bag, tied shut with a string. This little bag of treats was very special to every child and I can still remember the wonderful smell of peanuts and candy when opening it up.

Almost everyone in our church congregation was related in some way or another except for me and a small handful of neighbor kids. I can't say I really felt friended by any of the kids there and never felt like I fit in with them.

In springtime, when the school year was finished, we had bible school every day for a week in the church basement. I liked to draw and do crafts so it was fun for me. At the end of the week we put on a program and our parents were invited to attend. We had to memorize a bible verse, or put on a play, and show our parents all the little projects we'd been working on.

My cousins had their own nondenominational church just down the road from ours and invited me to attend their bible school also. I did go and enjoyed it, especially hanging out with my cousins. This church was different than mine and the preacher used scare tactics such as fiery pits of hell, to convince everyone they needed to be born again. Baptism was done only for older children and adults in a body of water unlike the Lutheran church I was brought up in where baptism is for newborn infants, a way to dedicate them to God and save them from going to hell in case they might die when young.

Catechism was mandatory in order to become a member of our Lutheran church so Mom made sure we all went. Classes were held during the school year in both 7th and 8th grade on Wednesday nights after school. By the time I was old enough to go to catechism there weren't enough kids in our neighborhood to hold the classes at our own church. Us Lutheran kids would walk to the Lutheran church in town after school and then get a ride home after the classes. Each parent was to take a turn driving us all home and although I was scared to death that my father would show up drunk when it was his turn, he never did. My mother must have really put her foot down on that issue. After we finished the two years of catechism or confirmation classes we were confirmed at a special church service. I was 13 when I was confirmed, the spring before my mother died. Shortly after my confirmation, Mom wrote a letter to her brother in Iowa. She told him that all of her children had now been confirmed and could follow what path they chose in life, she having done her part.

My church confirmation gown and red carnation

I don't remember my father coming to church with us at any time except for my sister's wedding. My aunt said that Grandpa had a falling out with the Lutheran church back in the 1940s when so many of the Lutheran churches split into different synods but I don't think this had anything to do with my father's avoidance of church. Dad never talked to me about religion or how he felt about it. I wish I would have asked him what he thought about it all, but I never did.

FUN AND FAMILY

I'm six years old and filled with excitement because my dad told me I could go fishing with him. We grab a tin can and wander around the yard and woods, upturning pieces of cast off lumber here and there to look for earthworms for bait. We have success underneath the boards on the shady trail that goes through the woods to the outhouse. Someone placed the old boards where the low spots are to keep our shoes out of the mud on rainy days. I carry the can filled with dirt and worms to the car and Dad loads up our poles. When we arrive a mile down the road at the little river I grab my cane pole and let Dad put a worm on my hook. I pitch that worm into the water with all the strength I can muster up and keep a watchful eye on my bobber. It dives under quickly so I jerk up my pole and run backwards up the bank as fast as I can, dragging a nice sucker up onto the brushy creek bank. We will have fish for supper tonight. It's a great spring day when the Juneberry trees are in blossom and the suckers and red horse are spawning. They will be boney but they'll taste much better than old venison.

In the summertime, before my sister left home she'd take the time to play outside with me. One of my favorite memories is of the time we took my dolls and doll furniture outside and we played "house" in the yard. One of my dolls was named Patsy. Patsy had adhesive tape wrapped around her neck to keep her head from falling off. She was a big, ugly, dirty doll with brown hair but I liked her because her eyes opened and shut. My favorite doll was a cheap little plastic one I named Jane, and she slept with me at night. I also had a "Tammy" doll that was a knock-off version of a Barbie doll. Her arms, legs, and head moved and I had lots of clothes for her. She was a special birthday or Christmas present given to me after I started grade school.

65

My "Tammy" doll also had a shiny black vinyl case to store her in with all her clothes. I also played with paper dolls. They came in a booklet and I cut the dolls out, along with many sets of clothing ,with a little blunt tipped safety scissors. Each piece of clothing had tabs on the edges of it and you had to be careful that you didn't cut those tabs off. You'd place a cut out dress over top the paper doll and then fold the tabs over the edges to hold it in place. Paper dolls were one of my favorite Christmas gifts.

Me playing "house" in the yard. The wooden doll bed was made by Grandpa Warner from Iowa.

I did a lot of things with paper when I was a kid. My brothers and I made paper airplanes. I'd cut colored construction paper in strips and glue them together making long paper chains. We would make origami paper finger games, with notes inside of them, at school. And in high school we played a lot of polish football, snapping with our finger a folded up triangular piece of paper back and forth across a table in the lunch room where we had study hall, scoring pretend touchdowns and kicking field goals.

In grade school I picked up some fads such as placing a large button on a string and pulling on the ends with both hands to make it spin. We also played a string finger game called "cats in the cradle". I took plastic lids from coffee cans or cool whip bowls and cut the centers out of them with a scissors. Then I attached a long string to the edge of the lid and tied a thread spool on the opposite end of the string for a weight. I'd stick my foot through the hole in the lid, bring it up around my ankle, and spin the string around in a circle, jumping over it with the other foot. Of course, jump ropes were a big deal too. We had ropes made of woven cloth with wooden handles attached.

Mom liked to do embroidery stitching on pillowcases, tablecloths, and small pieces of cotton fabric. She made gifts for others and for herself and she taught me how to do fancy stitches like French knots and flower petals. I loved embroidering and still do to this day as for me it is a small connection to my mom. She also mended jeans, patching the knees mostly. She mended socks by pulling them over a wooden darning egg with a handle on it that her father made. One of Mom's tricks was to remove a worn out collar from my father's flannel shirt, turn it around, and sew it back on. This way no one could see the frayed side as it was now upside down.

We kept Grandma Moeller's "Minnesota" treadle sewing machine in its wooden oak cabinet in the kitchen, but by the time I came along it wasn't used much anymore. The radio sat on top of the cabinet along with a flashlight and other things. As my friend Gil says, "Every flat surface was full," in our little house.

Following are three sayings my mom often repeated, just for fun. They're the only ones I can remember today. "If your nose itches you're going to kiss a fool." "If your palm itches you're going to come into money." "If you kill a spider it's going to rain." And Mom was always right!

Spending time with cousins who lived just a mile down the road was my favorite pastime in the summer. I would stay overnight at their houses and we'd talk and laugh all night if we could. It was an escape for me from my parents constant fighting. My dad's sister's family always had good food to eat and made sure you got plenty of it. My

Aunt Lydia would be cooking in the kitchen much of the time. She made wonderful stews, biscuits, apple and corn fritters, and used fresh lard for baking. Her two youngest kids, my cousins Ralph and Helen, were closer in age to me than my own sibs and we were pretty tight.

My cousin Helen and I would stay up late at night and listen to country music, sing, do jigsaw puzzles, and talk about everything under the sun. We were like sisters more than cousins. She was my rock as a child as she instilled good morals in me. She helped me find a stronger faith in God than I found through church, and got me interested in reading the bible. She also steered me in the right direction when it came to boys and having respect for myself.

My cousin inspired my interest in art and music. She was great at pencil sketches and she could sing very well and play guitar. Sometimes late at night she would strum her guitar and sing, and I'd sing harmony along with her. We both liked to write poetry. My mother subscribed to Grit newspaper, a weekly family newspaper from Iowa. One time I sent a poem to Grit that I had written for school about patriotism and it was published.

Aunt Lydia and Uncle Arvil were like my second parents and would do anything to help me at any time. They were the most generous, caring people I have ever known, the kind that would give you the coat off their backs. Their daughter, Paula, is this way still.

For a few years, at the end of summer, Uncle Bill (I liked to call him Bill, because William was actually his first name, Arvil his middle name) took his youngest kids, me included, to the Central Wisconsin State Fair at Marshfield. We rode on the Ferris Wheel and the tilt-a-whirl and spent the entire day eating fair food and playing different carnival games trying to win silly prizes. My dad would have never driven us to such a big event but he gave me some spending money.

I also hung out with my dad's brother, Uncle Axel's kids, for a few years while they lived in our township. They had a beautiful pond behind their house where we spent many hours swimming. The pond was surrounded by woods and had a soft sandy bottom with crystal clear water. We could see small pan fish swimming around us and feel them gently nibbling at our legs. The pond was shallow and we all felt safe in it. My cousins could swim like fish when very young and never had nor seemed to need any supervision while swimming.

We played Twister and other games at their house when I stayed overnight. One night when home alone, my cousins introduced me to their mom's No-doze pills. After downing a few, we giggled for what seemed like hours. It was the first and only time I tried any of the pills, but my cousins said they took them before. I didn't like the feeling and I never did that again.

Cousins: L to R back row: Susie holding Axel Jay, Paula, Helen; L to R front row: Tammy, Penny, Matt, & Me at a Family Reunion at Home

It seemed like this family never had much to eat and the oldest ones often had the task of taking care of the younger ones. Their mother was more interested in cigarettes and where she was going to get the money to buy them from, rather than putting food on the table. Often all we had to eat when I visited them were lettuce sandwiches. Uncle Axel was often gone all week working on road construction with my father.

Aunt Lois would shoo us outside to play for hours and lock the door so we couldn't get back in. She used her quiet time to clean the house, watch soaps on TV, or take a nap. One time I remember when she let us back into the house she went around picking up lint off the carpet and cursing her vacuum cleaner. She liked the soap opera that had the vampire in it, Barnabas Collins, called *Dark Shadows*. My mother wouldn't watch that soap opera and thought it was evil.

Aunt and Uncle drove a Cadillac with big fins on the back of it. I remember riding up to the local store with them in the huge Cadillac to buy gasoline. My aunt had just 29cents to spend on gas for that Caddy because the rest of her money went for cigarettes. They lived near us for about three years and then sold their home and moved back to Idaho where they had lived before. I was twelve when they left and my uncle gave me his piano. My dad's sister's family and my dad's brother's family had such a sharp contrast and difference in values but they were all family and I loved them all. They accepted my family just as it was too.

My Uncle Axel still inspires me today. He's an artist and musician and can always find the right words to make me smile.

I started riding bicycle when I was about ten or so. It gave me a new sense of freedom. I bought my first bike from Les when he outgrew it. It was a black boy's 20" bike and I learned to ride it by taking it up the hill in the yard by the big white pine tree. I'd hop on it and coast down that little hill and start pedaling until I got my balance. One day after I thought I had bicycling mastered I was heading down the driveway in front of my brothers when I wiped out and they ran over my knee while on their bikes. No bones were broken, but I was mad and hurting for quite a while.

Later I inherited a fancy gold 20" bike with high rise handlebars, a banana seat, and a sissy bar. It was a great bike with a three speed shifter on the bar ahead of the seat. I mounted a rearview mirror on the left handlebar so I could watch for upcoming cars without having to turn my head around, when going down the highway. If I did turn my head, my very long hair, which I never tied back, flew into my face and I couldn't see. The mirror worked great. I rode the bike to my cousins, to the local store and bar, and to the Sherwood Lake. When I was in high school I owned a few 26" 10 speed bikes with skinny tires on them.

My brother, Les, bought his first 26" bicycle for $8.00. In order to gather up enough money he saved his school lunch money from Mom. She gave him $1.25 a week, lunch cost a quarter a day. He went several weeks without eating until he saved up the money he needed. No one ever noticed he wasn't eating lunch and no one said much about the new bike either, but he reached his goal and got the bike!

My sister and older brothers all shared one bicycle for the most part. When my brother, Lynn, was about twelve years old he was hired out to work on a neighbor's farm for the summer, helping bale hay and other farm chores. His pay at the end of the summer was to be $1.00 a day and a brand new bicycle. Near summer's end another boy begin working with him and thought the work was too hard and quit, and talked my brother into quitting as well. Lynn had already received the bicycle but they took it back when he quit. He was paid for the days he had worked, but felt really awful about losing that new bike.

Some activities my siblings did were not only fun but also involved lots of hard work. In late winter they took on the art of making maple syrup, inspired no doubt by Grandpa Adam. This task was usually done in March when the temps thawed during the day but froze yet at nighttime. They would trudge through the deep but melting snow, gathering sap from tin buckets hung on cast iron spiles pounded into drilled holes in the maple trees in our woods. They fastened cheesecloth over the tops of milk cans with clothespins and poured the sap into the cans, straining out the dirt that way. The sap was stored in the milk cans until enough was gathered to boil it down. One time the sap boiled too long and started to burn in the sap pan. It crystalized into what looked like brown sugar and we sucked on it like hard candy. Whenever it was time to boil down sap, the smell when we hovered around the sap pan was wonderful.

Brother, Lynn, watching the sap pan cook down, in our woods.

I loved books when I was young and still do. We would get free books occasionally in the mail. They were always the beginning of a series of books or encyclopedias. Publishing companies hoped we'd like the first book in a series and then order the full set. I read those books over and over, and recall many subjects that started with an "A" and read all about aardvarks, anteaters, and Antarctica. We never bought any more of the books but at least we kept the "A" volumes!

I also liked to collect postage stamps and ordered cheap ones from foreign countries from the ads in the backs of comic books. I pasted them into a stamp album and learned a bit of geography.

HOLIDAYS

I don't remember much about Thanksgiving as a child other than drawing pictures of Pilgrims and Indians at school and talking about the great feast they had. Thanksgiving time was overshadowed by the annual whitetail gun deer hunt in our neck of the woods. Deer season was pretty much a long extended holiday in itself. Every November, when the whitetail gun deer season arrived, our neighborhood was buzzing with traffic, and the local taverns were packed.

Cousin Kiven, good friends Arnie and Duane, and others from southeastern Wisconsin stayed at Grandpa's cabin each year and hunted in our area. They were always more than welcome. Deer season was just as important and exciting as any other holiday at my house and it lasted a whole week long. Our hunters would bring treats like Brach's milk chocolate candy stars, sausage, and cheese and leave their leftovers with us when they went home. It was a time for rekindling old friendships, storytelling, and harvesting some much needed venison to help us make it through the winter. Deer season was, and for my family still is, a ritual that everyone looks forward to year after year but nowadays the old hunters are gone along with their stories and it is not the same to me.

Probably my favorite holiday as a child was Christmas. Of course we looked forward to the Christmas program at church that we planned weeks ahead of time. At home we put up a real evergreen tree most years. My brother, Vern, was usually the one who cut the tree down and brought it home. He'd often go down a gravel road not far from home and find the right tree on county land, a spruce tree usually. At that time no one cared and I never heard of anyone getting into trouble over it. We had many old ornaments and silver tinsel to decorate the tree with and the fresh piney smell of the Christmas tree in our house made it seem so special. The best part of Christmas was when my sister came home from Illinois for a few days. Mom and my brothers always looked forward to visiting with her.

Valentine's Day was fun at school. We were required to hand print names on cards for all the kids in our class. Sometimes we had close to 30 students in our homeroom. Each student made cardboard valentine card boxes, decorated them with colored construction paper, and cut slots in them. If lucky, I'd get a candy heart with a little message on it, along with the card. I'd also find out if any boys had their eye on me.

One special thing about Easter was having a new dress to wear to church. Later on I was allowed to wear it to school also. Mom and I would often order our new dresses from a mail order catalog. I don't remember decorating eggs but I do remember getting a basket filled with candy and a chocolate rabbit. My older brothers would hide a basket for me to find, and that never took too long, in our little house.

The 4th of July was special to me because often it was the only chance all summer I had to spend the day with my school friends. We watched the hometown parade together and caught candy thrown our way from the floats. We played games in the park and I stayed for the fireworks at night if I had a ride home. Dad liked to drink in the beer tent in the park and it was usually a scary ride home from town if it was with him. The 4th of July was one of those dreaded nights that we had to make sure Dad stayed awake and on his side of the highway all the way home. I remember so many times helping Dad walk from the car to the house, half propping him up, and leading the way. Dad would swear and laugh at the same time, all the way to the door.

VISITING GRANDMA EMMA

I'm nine years old and it seems to take forever to drive to central Iowa, six hours or more. We putz along the curvy highways and cross the Mississippi River near Prairie Du Chien. I feel frightened when we drive over the huge bridge and I cover my eyes with a pillow. Dad laughs at me. When I hear his laughter I'm no longer scared, just tickled to see him in a good mood. I hardly ever hear Dad laugh when he's not drunk. This is going to be a grand trip for Mom, Dad, and me. And Dad stays sober for the long drive!

Pleasant respites from woes at home summed up our summer trips to Eldora, Iowa, to visit my mom's mom and the only grandmother I ever knew, Grandma Emma Kewatt. Grandma lived on a dead end street at the edge of the small town of Eldora, and there was a huge field of corn growing close to her house. It was usually hot and muggy there in summertime and thunderstorms often rolled through in the night disturbing my sleep.

Mom packed her green suitcase and I packed my matching little red suitcase for the trip, suitcases Mom mail ordered from Fingerhut. Dad would drive Mom and I out to Grandma's home and leave us there in the middle of the summer for about three weeks. My brothers were old enough to stay home and kept busy working their summer jobs and my sister was out in the big world on her own.

Grandma had most of the modern conveniences. Her home was the same home that my mother grew up and lived in until she married my dad when she was 30.

Grandma Emma Kewatt, Mom, and me, at Grandma's Iowa home. Grandma grew many flowers and had a goldfish pond in her front yard in the summertime. Grandma told me she felt unwanted as a child. She said her German parents were "old" when they had her, had journeyed to America with what they thought was a full family, only to have another child come along, after settling in Iowa. I don't know if that is what made her seem to be a bit of a sour person. Maybe she didn't feel good at times, or felt saddened after becoming a widow in her '50s and thought life dealt her an unfair blow, as I often thought she appeared to be a bit unhappy. Her husband, Grandpa Warner Kewatt, died suddenly of a heart attack not long after my parents were married in 1945. Grandma Emma was a survivor, and a stubborn German just like me.

Grandma Emma's home in Eldora, Iowa, in the 1960s

I had my own bedroom at Grandma's house and quickly unpacked my clothes and hung them in a real closet. In Grandma's bedroom against the wall stood an antique bathtub with claw feet that I could soak in. Staying at my grandmothers was a wonderful escape from reality but I will admit that I did get a little homesick. I missed our Wisconsin trees, as that part of Iowa was filled with what seemed like endless fields of corn and very few forests.

A distant older cousin, Lori, lived across the street from Grandma. She was kind to me and took me for walks downtown and swims in the city pool. City swims were different than country swims. I had to wear a rubber cap on my head with all my hair tucked inside so that it wouldn't get caught in the pool drain. The chlorine in the water hurt my eyes and stunk to high heaven, but it was fun anyway.

Grandma gave me gloves to wear when I picked goose berries off the thorny bushes in her back yard. She made the most delicious pies with those strange looking green berries. Grandma was an excellent cook. She always wore dresses and aprons when she cooked, and so did Mom when at home.

There were pretty dishes in Grandma's wooden cupboards between the living room and dining room that were built-in by my grandpa. There were cobalt blue dishes and glasses in those cupboards with see through glass doors. I think that is why I like cobalt blue glassware to this day.

Mom and Grandma loved to sit at the table and play cards. I played "500 Rummy", and "Go Fish" with them. We also played "Concentration" and "Solitaire". On one visit, Grandma gave me a pretty gold ring with an amethyst stone in it and I still have it.

Grandma could talk German but I don't remember hearing or learning much of the language. There are just three of Grandma's German phrases still stuck in my head and the only one that makes sense yet is "doonder und blitzen" or "thunder and lightning". When Mom was young she was encouraged to speak English at home and to forget the German language. During World War I, anything that would reflect a German heritage was unpopular. Mom was born in 1914, the year the "Great War" began.

Grandma didn't like my father and often nagged about how rough he made my mother's life. Of course he resented her words and actions and didn't care for her either. Grandma was chubby; she was also a "stubborn German" as my father called her and she had a tough skin about her. She was a faithful church goer, attending the Lutheran Church in Eldora. She was very active with church groups and women's clubs that took turns monthly entertaining in each other's homes. There was a large separation in the community between the Lutherans and the Catholics. They had their own cemeteries, and you wouldn't even consider dating someone who was of a different faith.

We were fortunate that we got to spend the little time we did with Grandma Emma in Iowa. I only remember her coming to visit us once at home when I was very young. My father would get angry about the amount of water she used to wash dishes with, etc.

Usually when we visited Grandma we spent at least one day at my mother's sister's home, Aunt Geraldine, who lived nearby in a little town called New Providence, Iowa. N. P. was only about a twenty minute drive from Grandma's. Aunt Geraldine was the opposite of my mother in that she had a wonderful husband, a modern and well-kept home, plenty of money, and two perfect children. At least that's the way it seemed.

Aunt Jeri, as she preferred to be called, was ten years younger than Mom, and had a twin brother, Gerald. I'd say she and Gerald were as different as night and day as Gerald liked to drink and Jeri was a teetotaler. Aunt Jeri would cook a large meal for us and set the table properly with cloth napkins, matching plates, and silverware. Pastel colored aluminum drinking cups each filled to the brim with water, and a matching aluminum water pitcher, always sat on the table. Everything was just so. When at home, we never drank water with our meals and I wondered why anyone would do such a thing when I saw those tall water glasses on Aunt Jeri's table.

Aside from the awkwardness I felt in her orderly home, Aunt Jeri was kind to me. I imagine she pitied my mother and me, but I didn't get that message from her. I really didn't see her often enough to become close to her and I never knew her children. They were grown up and gone from home already when I came to visit. Her husband, Uncle Dean, was hard of hearing. He was very kind to me and always winked and made me smile. He was tall and handsome and one time he took me to his cousin's farm to ride their Shetland pony.

When I was 13, we made our last visit to Grandma's house when my mother was very sick from cancer in the spring of 1973. It wasn't a happy time then but it was an important trip for Mom. It was even uncertain if she could make the trip as she only weighed about 80 lbs. and was becoming very frail before we left home. Mom was able to see her sister and both of her brothers, Gerald and Lawrence, on that trip. They said their goodbyes in their minds but not out loud. Mom passed away a few weeks later.

A year and a half later Grandma Emma passed away at Eldora in early 1975. My father drove my brothers and I to the funeral to say good-by to her. Later my siblings and I inherited about $600.00 each from her estate (dividing six ways what would have been our mother's portion).

79

I got a penny less than the rest because I was the youngest. Isn't it silly that I remember that!

FAMILY REUNIONS

Our family reunions were centered around my paternal Grandfather Adam Moeller's birthdays. He was born July 30, 1876, in Jackson County, Iowa, oldest son of sixteen children, thirteen who grew to adulthood. Everyone gathered in Grandpa's yard, our yard too, in the shade near his log cabin, for a huge potluck picnic and a good old visit. My Grandpa's brothers would drive up from Iowa as long as they were able to, bringing their fiddles with them. It was fun to see them all playing music together and enjoying one another's company.

Our Moeller reunions were filled with cousins from nearby and from Iowa and Illinois. We played outside all day and it was the most fun, something to look forward to all year long. I don't remember a reunion day that it rained! There was plenty to eat as everyone brought food and there was always a large birthday cake for Grandpa too, with candles on it. I still enjoy looking at old photos of those reunions from the 1960s. My best memory was of the reunion where my Aunt Theresa made Grandpa's 90th birthday cake. She baked two sheet cakes, cut out a "9" and a "0" and put them side by side. We all watched Grandpa blow out his candles.

That may have been the reunion when Great Uncle Paul Moeller, from Iowa, brought me a very special gift. He opened up the trunk of his car and lifted out a miniature log cabin that he had hand crafted. The cabin had a door that opened and even curtains in the windows. It had a carved brick fireplace chimney and a roof that I could lift off to put things inside of it. I treasured the little cabin and still have it today. Great Uncle Paul lived in southeastern Iowa with his wife and two sons, Virgil, who passed away at a young age, and Paul Jr. I named my son after Great Uncle Paul.

I also have fond memories of Great Uncle Henry Moeller and Great Uncle Gustave Moeller coming to our family reunions. Henry would throw dimes on the ground for the little kids to gather and Gustave had a glass eye that he would pop out on occasion.

This is a favorite photo of one of our many Moeller family reunions at home with Grandpa Adam, his cane across his lap, taken in 1961. I guess someone had the idea that we should all cross our arms. Back row L to R: Lynn, Vern, Jack, Judy, Kent, Paula, Helen standing in front of Neda, Marla. Front row L to R: Grandpa, Michael, Les, Ralph, and my little self, standing behind Ralph.

When Grandpa Adam's arthritis and cataracts made it hard for him to walk and see, our family reunions ceased for many years. He was the glue that kept our large family together.

Thankfully we have been able to keep the family reunions going once again at Sherwood Park each July.

When I was five years old, Great Uncle Paul Moeller made and gave me this little log cabin on his visit from Iowa to our family reunion.

I'VE GOT MAIL!

When Grandpa Adam was living with Aunt Theresa in Illinois I would write letters to him when I was young. I also wrote to Grandma Emma in Iowa and several great aunts and uncles. Letter writing was very important back then. It was something you did on a regular basis if you wanted to keep in touch with family and friends, especially when you didn't have a telephone or couldn't afford to make long distance calls very often.

My mother always told me, "If you don't put a letter in the mailbox the mailman won't bring you any letters." I took that statement literally as a child and thought maybe it was a rule made by our own mailman from Pittsville.

I also wrote letters to Marla in Illinois and I wrote to Lynn and Vern when they were away in the Army. It was always so good to hear back from all of them.

In Grandpa's opinion, sending a birthday card or a Christmas card with just a signature was a sin, or pure laziness. If you couldn't take the time to write a message then you shouldn't bother sending a card at all.

I was about five when I started writing letters and took those daily walks with my mother to our mailbox, always hoping for a letter back in return. Getting the mail each day was a big event.

My mother was a great letter writer. If she needed to send a quick message to my Aunt Lydia, before she had a telephone, she would jot a note down on a postcard or letter and place it in the mailbox with "Please Drop" written on the front. The mailman would then scribble over the stamp with a pen (so it couldn't be used again) and put the postcard in Lydia's mailbox a mile down the road the same day.

Dear Grandpa,
How are you? In school we
will learn how to write pretty soon.
It snowed at our ~~a~~ place
today. Today in school we got
to take our reading books
home the best ~~story~~ storie we
read was "The magic show."
I got my front teeth all the
way in. Last night I got all
my valentines made for school.
A couple of days ago ~~a~~ a boy
in are room in school fall on
the ice and broke his collar bone
he is my friend his name is
Douglas Urban.

Love your grandchild

Kay MacVoe

NEIGHBORS

I'm opening gifts at my first wedding shower. My neighbors put the shower on for me and have set out a tasty lunch with cake, coffee and punch. I take the lid off a small white gift box to find a snazzy aluminum paring knife wrapped carefully in white tissue paper. The lady who gifted it tells me that she sells these knives in several sizes as a fund raiser for her church... but this one has the tip broken off of it, so it can't be sold. I still have the knife in my silverware drawer to this day, it is one of my favorites, and I haven't had to sharpen it in over thirty years.

When I was very young, around the corner to the north on Hwy 73 lived our neighbors; Elmer, Dolly and Albert. Albert was the son, in his thirties, destined to live a life with his parents due to his slow nature. My brothers were friends with Albert and they nicknamed him "bubble-eyes", but they meant no harm. Albert reminded me of the comic strip character my father always read on the back page of his daily newspaper, the Marshfield News-Herald, called "Alley Oop".

Elmer and Dolly were goodhearted and they would often give Mom a ride to town in their huge old car when she needed something. Mom and I would sit in the back seat gazing out the windows on the way to town; I with my nose plugged as Dolly had a bit of an odor. Most of the time Elmer wore a felt hat and he looked a lot like Jed Clampett from the Beverly Hillbillies.

Albert brought us fresh milk from his milk cows from time to time. It was a nice gesture, but the milk had manure floating on the surface now and then, and I couldn't force myself to drink it. When he came to visit, Albert would barrel through the door of our house and grab the water bucket dipper for a drink. After he slobbered all over that dipper

I hesitated to use it myself for a very long time. Maybe he had diabetes and that's why he was so thirsty. I never knew what became of Albert, Dolly, and Elmer, when they moved away. But they were good neighbors, the kind you don't forget.

The Z. family owned the local bar and grocery store when I was young and it was a handy place in our community. Mom would buy groceries there sometimes and Dad "lived" there on weekends and drank lots of beer there. At least it wasn't far from home so he generally was able to drive back to the house without getting in trouble. Mom and I would go with him sometimes too. When we ordered pizza at the bar it always tasted delicious as we had no way to bake a pizza at home. Mr. and Mrs. Z. were good to me and amazingly patient with my dad who was there so often. Dad always paid for everything in cash. He wasn't one to charge or start up a bar bill and I'd say he was a good customer.

A mile and half east of us lived a friend of my dad named Davey who was a Navy veteran of WWII. Davey was the local car fix-it man and he had a little garage loaded with tools, a hoist, a tire changer and balancer, you name it. Davey could fix just about anything and he never charged very much either. He was a bachelor, raised by his mother's parents after his mom died when he was quite young. When Davey's grandparents passed he inherited their farm and remained there the rest of his life fixing cars, tractors, lawn mowers, etc.

A friend of my sister bought Davey's farm after he passed away. In a bedroom of the old abandoned house Davey grew up in, (he had since moved into a trailer house nearby), were many sets of trousers, shirts, and dresses on hangers. The clothes belonged to Davey's grandparents and although they'd been gone more than fifty years it seemed as though he'd been waiting for them to come back home. It gave me a feeling of sadness I can't explain.

Mrs. S., a lady who lived a few miles down the road, used to mow the cemetery when I was young, which was right across from our driveway. One time my father was walking out to get his mail when he caught Mrs. S. going through our mailbox. Although she was a church friend of my mother, she had a reputation for being very nosey.

And she also had a reputation for "milking the system" or mowing the cemetery more than needed to make herself some extra money. I liked Mrs. S. but there was something about the way she talked. She always sounded like she had a wad of cotton in her mouth. She was a pretty good friend to my mother and always reminded me of how much she thought of Mom after she passed. Mom said Mrs. S. met Mr. S., many years her senior, when they each came to look at a home that was for sale in our township at the same time. They both fell in love with the home so decided to buy it together, get married, and try to fall in love with each other. Others have different versions of this story but I like my mom's best.

My mother went to Ladies Aid, a church group that had meetings once a month at different people's houses. She enjoyed the group and it gave her a chance to socialize. Of course my mother never entertained the ladies at our house. When it was her turn she used the church basement. We saw many of our neighbors in church but really didn't mingle with them elsewhere. Sometimes I got the feeling we just didn't fit in. And honestly, we really didn't.

PETS

I'm twelve and some friends of my dad have brought their little son over to our place to see my pet deer fawn. I cup my hands together and holler out her name, "Brambly, Brambly", and within a short time she comes running to me from the nearby woods. She is happy to see me and I reach in my pocket to pull out an apple. Brambly licks my hand and then begins to lick the little boy's ear while he giggles.

When I was quite young my brothers had hound dogs for coon hunting, etc. They were big, hyper dogs, and not very kid friendly. The dog I remember most was named Rowdy. She often ran loose around our yard and was a pretty nice dog. We had cats now and then but none in the house and they were never very tame. I also had a few pet rabbits and my first one was a gift at Easter time when I was 10 or eleven. I had a cage that sat up off the ground on posts covered in chicken wire with a roof over top to keep the bunnies sheltered.

When I was twelve my brother, Vern, cornered a tiny doe fawn between a couple fences in the woods near our house and carried it home in his arms. The fawn's mother had been killed by a car not far from our place on the highway. Our neighbors had already rescued the buck twin. We named our doe fawn, Brambly, and she was the nicest pet I ever had.

I kept Brambly in our house at first and she slept on a blanket on the kitchen floor at night. Mom didn't like having her in the house but she didn't complain too much. This little doe fawn was a very smart animal. I fed her milk from a baby bottle every few hours the first month or so. At first I mixed powdered milk with water for her bottle to save money but that didn't set well with her tummy so I then bottle fed her store bought whole milk. She quickly learned how to lap water with her tongue and to browse on grass and clover in our yard.

When Brambly wanted to go outside she would wiggle the door knob with her nose and do the same thing when she wanted to come back in our house. If I was in bed when she needed to go outside, she would lick my face and wake me up. She never made a mess on the floor and was pretty much housebroken right from the start.

We would feed Brambly apples and make her beg by standing on her hind legs for them. She liked to lick my hands, ears, and bunt or push hard against my arm over and over when she was hungry for a bottle of milk.

Many people came to visit her that summer. Later on we kept her in the shed or Grandpa's empty cabin at night but let her lose during the day. She never traveled far but would occasionally venture from our large yard into the woods. Whenever I clapped my hands and called her name she'd always come running... except for one time!

Here Brambly and I stand out in our "field" not far from the house in 1972. Behind me are hay bales my brothers used for backstops while target practicing with their bow and arrows. I have an apple in my hand.

One late spring day two game wardens came to the house and wanted to take Brambly away. I was home alone at the time, and scared, so at their insistence I called for her several times and clapped my hands wildly, but she didn't come. At the time I was doing all this I was also crying my eyes out at the thought of losing my pet. The wardens told me when I found her that I should tie her up or lock her in the shed and call them right away. They told me they'd come back to get her and put her in the Stanley Zoo, about fifty miles northwest of my home.

I had no idea where Stanley was, or if the town even had a zoo, but it wasn't long after the wardens left that Brambly appeared, so I quickly locked her up in the cabin. When my brother came home from work he was very upset about the whole deal and told me to let her out and forget about calling the wardens. When Dad came home that Friday night from his job he was really upset about the warden affair. He too, was adamant about not contacting the game wardens. Dad was quite attached to Brambly, just as I was.

The next day we had to go to town to do our usual laundry chores and grocery shop. Just in case the wardens returned, Dad wrote a note addressed to them and stuck it on the house door. He told them they had been trespassing, harassing his minor daughter, and how they shouldn't bother to come back to our place. I never saw the wardens again.

Brambly hung around all that summer and fall and she was a great joy to me. When the leaves were falling off the trees, several times she brought other young deer up to the house with her. During the gun deer season I tied orange ribbons around Brambly's neck to help protect her from being shot. One of our resident deer hunters said he saw her running with a group of deer, her orange collar flapping in the breeze, while he was out hunting back of our home.

When the snow came we kept a large bale of hay out in front of the house and Brambly would nibble on it sometimes and make her bed in it at night. In February of that winter she wandered to the east one day and never returned. I followed what I thought were her tracks in the snow as far as I could, but I didn't find her. She was healthy when she left so I like to think she joined up with a group of local deer and returned to the wild. I felt unbelievably sad to have lost the best pet I'd ever had, but was thankful for the awesome experience I had in raising her.

On my 16th birthday my brother, Vern, took me several miles from home to pick out a puppy from a friend of a friend. We were riding on his motorcycle so I tucked the little female dog that I picked out of the litter inside my jacket and the three of us rode home. She was part Spitz and beagle and we named her Junco after the little black and gray birds that frequented our yard in winter. I let Junco have one batch of pups, Dad kept the runt of the litter, and then I had her spayed. I kept Junco for ten years, my only pet dog really, until she passed. She was a very timid dog and was extremely well behaved.

A second fawn came into my life shortly after I got Junco. A man from a neighboring county brought the fawn to us in the back seat of his car. He said he caught the deer after it's mother had been struck by a car. He remembered my dad, having met him in a tavern somewhere, and heard that we had raised a fawn before. Dad said the man was an ex-con. I wasn't sure what an ex-con was, but I didn't think it was a good thing to be.

My new pet was also a doe fawn but she was not as smart as Brambly. We named her "Flag" and she and Junco became good friends. They chased each other in circles in the yard and played together. I am quite sure Flag thought she was a dog too.

Flag stayed around until early fall and then disappeared. Such is life, but raising fawns was an experience I will never forget. After the loss of my mother, Brambly was especially a comfort and a diversion for me. I considered her a gift from God.

Flag and Junco were best friends to each other, and to me.

My brother caught a young crow one spring, I'm not really sure how, but we had it for a pet one whole summer. My dad loved that crow, too. I guess he had a soft spot for pets. Dad would be walking across the yard and the crow would land on his shoulder and stay perched there as he strolled along. Eventually the crow would crap down the back of Dad's shirt, but he'd just laugh about it. One day we found the crow lying dead in the yard under the highline wire and assumed it was electrocuted.

Dad always wanted to find a sand hill crane egg and try to hatch it. He had a burning desire to raise a crane after reading a magazine article about someone who had done so, but never got the chance.

Another pet that I had for a very short time, but can't forget, was a baby skunk. I read about a place near Neshkoro, Wisconsin, that sold descented skunks for pets and I talked Dad into letting me buy one for $25.00, with my own money. We drove about 80 miles to pick up that skunk. It was quite an extraordinary feat for my father to drive that far on a whim, but he was very supportive of the idea.

My pet turned out to be a male skunk and I named him Jesse. I put him in one of our old rabbit cages feeling he'd be safe and comfortable there. I only had the skunk one week when one night I forgot to lock the door of the cage and the next morning he was gone; the door was open. I found Jesse in the yard, dead, lying underneath one of my brother's old cars. It appeared as if he'd been choked in the neck. I thought maybe another wild male skunk killed him after reading that male skunks are quite territorial.

Losing my pet skunk was quite a letdown, but I never got another one as skunks were too expensive, and Neshkoro was too far away.

WHEN CANCER FIRST CAME INTO MY LIFE

I'm 11 and I'm sitting on the makeshift couch in the "living room" watching television with my mother but my memories of that day are not of the show we were watching. They are of Mom clutching her left breast in pain. The pain was probably rated a number ten, from the look on her face. I saw her in pain before, but never as much as on this day. In my child turned to grownup voice I told her I thought she should see a doctor. But she didn't want to. She hoped the pain would just go away. It didn't.

That summer my sister, Marla, came home for a visit. When she noticed too what was going on, she talked Mom into going to our local clinic for a checkup. Within days of the visit, Mom was in the hospital having surgery. They called her procedure a radical mastectomy (the surgery left a crater, a literal dip there in her chest) and along with her breast they removed most of the lymph nodes under her left arm. I had never heard of breast cancer before. It wasn't talked about in public or on TV like today. Cancer was something other people had in other worlds, not in my world. I asked if Mom would be home for my birthday and they said maybe, but she wasn't. They told me everything was going to be o.k.

I didn't feel like going back to school that fall. My mom went to the clinic in Marshfield regularly for cobalt treatments. She lost her hair and suffered quite a bit, but she never complained to me. Her arm began to swell from the pit to her hand. I could tell it gave her a lot of pain as she rubbed it and cried often. We talked a lot, Mom and I. We talked about girl things. We talked about the day I would get married. When I think back on it, she was preparing me as best she could for when she couldn't, but I didn't realize it until many years later.

There wasn't any chemotherapy back then. I don't know if the cobalt treatments really helped her but I suppose they gave her more time. About a year later, she had surgery again for cancer that eventually spread to her stomach. Surgeons removed most of her stomach and it seemed she was in the hospital for a few months in the summertime.

We went to see her as often as we could. The hospital was 25 miles away from our home in a town we had seldom driven to before all this. Dad drove in with me on weekends and my brothers and I would drive in when we could during the week. After our hospital visits, Mom would give us a little money so that we could go to Chips, a little fast food place, and buy hamburgers and French fries. To this day I hate eating at Chips but at the time those hamburgers were a real treat. I don't know where Mom found spending money to give us but I suppose she got it from Dad.

After her stomach surgery, Mom lost so much weight and then several months later the cancer spread to the bone in her thigh. Her leg was very painful and it was hard for her to walk. She had radiation treatments on her leg and I remember the black "x" her doctor put on her skin to mark the spot. She lost her hair and wore a wig.

Les and I would take her to the big clinic downtown in Marshfield for her doctor appointments. He was 16 then and had just gotten his license so he could do the driving. I helped Mom with house work, laundry, and buying groceries. She needed someone to hang onto for support when she walked and would take hold of my arm. It was near the end when we took our last trip to Iowa to visit Grandma Emma.

My sister came home that summer when things were getting pretty bad. One night Mom couldn't pee and was really suffering. She kept asking for more pain pills, prescription morphine, but the pills didn't work anymore. She only weighed about 75 pounds. We called the ambulance that night to come and take her to the hospital. I didn't want to ride along, but I did go up to visit her once she was situated in her hospital bed. She told me when I saw her not to worry and said she would be coming home tomorrow. I thought she would, and I think she did too, but she didn't. My sister, I, and Aunt Lydia, who

94

lived a mile down the road, sat up all night that night talking in our kitchen. We got the call from the hospital about 3:00 a.m. that Mom had passed.

Dad was away at work on the road somewhere when Mom died. He had talked it over with Mom that Sunday night before he left for his job. They decided it didn't matter too much if he was home or gone so figured he might as well go to work that week. One thing I remember about that Sunday night before Dad left was that it was the first and only time I heard them say they loved each other. It made me feel warm inside to hear that. I never saw them hug or kiss ever. But there was something there, some real love perhaps buried for a long time that resurfaced that last night they were together. I'm so glad I overheard their conversation as I slept in my little bed not far from theirs.

I didn't want to cry in front of anybody. I didn't want to cry at the funeral. I knew if I started I wouldn't be able to stop so I went out to the outhouse and I cried my eyes out there, many times. The outhouse was far enough away from the house so it was my refuge, a place to go for privacy, strange as that may sound.

I was 13 the summer that my mom passed; I turned 14 a month later. It was hard for me because although I knew how sick my mother was I didn't think she would actually die. Not long before passing she told me she had always wondered why I came along in her later life but said that now she knew the reason. It was because I was meant to be her caretaker and we'd get through this mess and everything would be o.k. Other people lost family members but they were people I didn't really know. I just didn't think it could happen in my world. But here I was... without my mom and feeling so very alone.

My brother, Vern, got a leave to come home from the Army where he'd been stationed in Germany for Mom's funeral. He took it very hard but he didn't say much. He didn't want to go back to Germany afterward because he hated Army life. I put my thinking cap on and came up with a plan, a plan that would allow him to stay home a little longer. I took a big swallow to get rid of my fear and I called the Red Cross on our phone at home. I had the contact information because we had called the Red Cross to let him know how sick Mom was hoping they'd let him come home before it was too late. I told the person I spoke to on the phone (acting anonymously) that his mother had passed away and he was needed at home to take care of his young sister, because his father was away working on road construction for the summer. I never said who I was and they never asked me but they told me his leave would be extended an extra six to eight weeks. My brother seemed pleased and I think he needed that extra time at home.

When Vern did go back to Germany it was pretty lonely for me at home but by then I was back in school. Dad was still working on the road and away from home during the week until cold weather halted construction projects so I was home alone a lot. My aunt and uncle were always there for me and I stayed with them overnight whenever I wanted to. They were good to help me with school things or give me rides when I needed them and they took care of me when I was sick.

Life went on. I grew up fast, and had plenty of independence in my teen years. Dad kept drinking, but there was something different about my relationship with him. Although we argued a lot when I was a teen we actually were forced to communicate and so I began to realize that he was an o.k. person, not the evil, uncaring father I thought he was. The older I grew, the better we got along, and I am grateful that I got to know him before it was too late.

I'm feeling a bit guilty here like I've been too hard on my dad in my reflections of life at home and life with him in my writings. I want to stress that Dad was a very smart man, and he cared about all of his kids. He was as honest as the day is long. And when I became an adult I grew to love him dearly and always felt that love from him in return. He did the best he could.

I think now about how I never knew my mother as an adult would know their parent but I have good memories of her. She was always kind and thoughtful and caring. We sang songs together, played cards together; she taught me how to sew and embroidery. We talked about boys and how women get moody and lots of little things. I regret now how difficult her life was with such poor living conditions and my father's drinking. But she didn't complain that much really, just accepted things and stayed as strong as she could. She always looked about 10 years younger than her age and never had a gray hair until she started her cancer treatments. I'm thankful I had as much time with her as I did.

KINDNESS

Many people turn their backs on those who are less fortunate or troubled but there were a few people that made a difference or left a favorable impression on me during my early teenage years and I want to mention them and the kindness they showed me.

When I was twelve or thirteen, Mr. and Mrs. D., from the neighboring township, started up a youth group for local kids and I was invited to join. We met once a month, usually at their house, and had lots of great treats to eat and fun activities planned. Mrs. D. drove out to pick me up and take me back home even though they lived several miles away. The D.'s had two sons about my age and I think they intended this to be a good experience for their children as well. They were religious and so we said prayers and had some sort of bible lessons at the meetings, but they were not pushy with anyone about religion. We also had different activities that we did together with the group. One of them was tobogganing at Power's Bluff Park. The whole youth group experience was very nice. The D.'s were so kind to kids and thoughtful to share their home and time. She was a teacher and he was a farmer.

My cousin Judy and her husband, a doctor, invited me to stay with them for 3 weeks at their home in Dubuque, Iowa, when I was about fourteen. They were kind to me, took me shopping and let me pick out new clothes for school in exchange for babysitting their young kids. It was fun trying so many new clothes on and shopping at a big department store. They took me for a small airplane ride while my cousin's husband was taking flying lessons. It was quite scary as he did a required engine stall in midair and the plane did a quick nosedive. I hung on for dear life and survived the flight. I came back home to the Wisconsin woods feeling a little more grown up, a little more cultured.

My sister took me to her Illinois home to hang out for a few weeks at a time during the summers while I was in high school. It was good to get away from home and be around people and not be so alone.

One time I took the Greyhound bus myself to Rockford, Illinois, where my sis was to come and pick me up at the bus station. As I sat in the little building in Rockford, I watched people coming and going and waited for my sister. I was intrigued and amused by what seemed like an army of overweight women who marched in and sat in chairs against the wall with little black and white television sets attached to each chair arm. In order to view the T.V.'s you had to drop a quarter in a slot atop them and then they'd play for a set number of minutes. It appeared that the women were coming in to view a soap opera. They were each armed with their own personal bag of donuts and a handful of quarters which kept them entertained for quite some time. As I sat there watching them a black man walked in wearing a purple velvet blazer and matching hat and seated himself across from me. He motioned with his index finger for me to come over by him and his white teeth were shining through his smiling lips. I was terrified and clung to the handle of my large suitcase in front of me and stared at the floor. I don't know when the black man or the fat ladies watching T.V. left the station. I kept to myself, scared to death, and kept my head down until my sister arrived.

My handsome cousin, Michael, was two years older than me and lived near my sister. Once when I visited my sis, Michael took me bowling for the first time. I did pretty well and I think I beat him. He took me to Burger King and bought me my first Whopper and it was so big I couldn't eat it all. He was a kind and caring cousin that I won't forget who went on to be an Illinois state wrestling champion contender, and an airplane mechanic after graduating from Urbana College. Michael tragically passed away at 27 from esophageal cancer. It makes me wonder how cancer decides who it's going to grab ahold of.

GROWING UP

I didn't get my driver's license until just before my senior year at the age of 17, but that was soon enough. I bought a Ford Maverick just like my dad's car but it was a couple years older than his and not as fancy. I asked my brother, Lynn, to check it out first and see if it was an o.k. deal. The Maverick was a trusty car for me. One of my big ventures with it was to drive several friends to a concert in Wausau to see the Ozark Mountain Dare Devils in our senior year of high school.

As soon as I bought the car I was able to drive to Pittsville on Saturdays by myself and buy the weekly groceries and do the laundry. Thankfully there was no more time wasted in having to search for my dad in the taverns afterward. This was bliss! I didn't mind the chore of doing this at all, it gave me a new sense of freedom.

My brother, Vern, was discharged and came home from the Army when I was in high school (after being stationed in Germany) and we became close. Many times when I was sick or needed a note for school he would write one up for me as Dad was often away from home on a job. My brother and I went for motorcycle rides. On a couple of my birthdays he took me to Saddle Mound and we spent the day climbing it and exploring.

Vern didn't have a driver's license to drive a car but he did have a license to drive a motorcycle. Back then you could have one or the other, you didn't need to have the car license first to get the motorcycle license. He had taken a test in Neillsville in high school for his driver's license but didn't pass. I think it traumatized him enough that he was afraid to try the test again. Before I planned to move away from home after graduating from high school I made sure he got his car driver's license. I asked my uncle if he would take Vern for his test at a little town where I took mine, and he aced it. I knew he would because he was a very good driver.

I guess you could say at this point I was not a kid anymore. My circumstances early in life caused me to grow up fast. In my senior year of high school I had my own car, managed my own finances, began dating my first husband Mike, …. and the world was a pretty good place to be!

The last two years of my teen life were filled with both happiness and sadness. I lost my brother, Vern, from injuries he suffered in a motorcycle accident the summer after I graduated from high school. He'd been drinking and lost control of his bike about ten miles from home. It was a hard time for Dad and I. Vern had been depressed ever since he came home from the Army and I didn't know how to help him cope. No one really knew how much he was suffering and his death was a real tragedy for our family.

A few months after we lost Vern, I married Mike, had a handsome baby boy, and was widowed when our son was just five weeks old. Tragically, I lost my first husband in another motorcycle accident. It was sudden, no time to prepare for such a loss, and left me feeling as though I'd been torn in two. I thought I had a plan, I thought my whole life was falling into place, and then I had to start all over again.

With the death of my mother to cancer and the death of my brother and first husband, some of the closest people to me in my young life, all in just a few short years, I wasn't sure how to carry on. I had a little talk with Dad one day when I came to visit him and he told me something that has stuck with me to the present. I said, "Dad, did you ever feel that life wasn't worth living anymore?" His immediate, short, and simple answer was, "Don't ever let yourself get that low." Dad's quick response seemed to make perfect sense. I have never held my head down that far again, and I hope I can keep my chin up through this new cancer mess that has encompassed my own life now.

PART TWO

I wrote this poem when I noticed how my cat, Fred, keeps looking over his shoulder when he eats from his dish. He's leery, afraid, and can't stop looking over that shoulder. I've realized that I am often just like my cat when I worry about cancer returning. I'm doing the same thing, maybe nonsensically, but I can't help it.

OVER YOUR SHOULDER

You keep looking over your shoulder,
Thinking it's near, it'll soon be here.
Your heart beats faster
And you keep looking...
Over your shoulder.

Wondering when your time will come,
When you'll hear the news, win or lose,
When the darkness will appear,
So you keep looking...
Over your shoulder.

Time keeps ticking, as you keep looking,
Wondering when, thinking then,
So much time wasted,
As you keep looking...
Over your shoulder.

If you'd look ahead and not behind
Quit collecting, stop reflecting,
But fear rules your emotions,
So you keep looking...
Over your shoulder.

THE BIG "C" AND ME

I'm sitting in the doctor's office getting my annual physical. I'm twenty-something. My doctor asks about my family history and I tell her about my mother's breast cancer. She says "How old was your mother when she was diagnosed?" I tell her, "56". And then I tell her Mom didn't make it. It seems like I do this every year because the doctors keep asking that same question.

Because of my mom's breast cancer I had my first baseline mammogram at the age of 38, which I believe now was overkill. Then at age 40, I started getting annual mammograms. At first they were scary, but then as the years went by the tests became routine and just a nuisance more or less. But then when I was 52, after having a few biopsies through the years, a mass was found on my left breast that caused me a great deal of anxiety. It was precancerous but when removed with outpatient surgery all the margins around it were clear. I felt both terrified and ecstatic when I learned that it had been caught early and I didn't need any further treatment. I was offered a chemo pill called tamoxifen to prevent full blown breast cancer from coming my way and the plan involved taking it for five years. It was such an easy choice to take this little pill as I wanted to do everything in my power to prevent having to go through the hell that my mother did. I hastily and eagerly answered questions in a lengthy survey and filled that prescription. A genetic test later revealed that I had no known genetic mutations to predispose me to breast cancer, but what I had been through with Mom still made me want to take those pills.

After about a month on tamoxifen I became nauseated and could hardly eat for a week. I went back to see the surgeon at a scheduled six week checkup and he suggested I stop the tamoxifen for two or three days and then if I felt better to start back up with it. I did this, and I did start feeling better so continued back on the prescription again.

Now and then that following spring and summer I had small sharp pains in my sides and lower belly, and I attributed the pains to tamoxifen. I often felt full a little quicker than normal when I ate. I didn't give much thought about what I considered these "little things" going on with my health. I wasn't going to let some small issues stop me from taking a drug that might be giving me these side effects but yet spare me from getting breast cancer.

When I had my annual physical in September of 2012 my family practice doctor said, to put it bluntly, "Your uterus feels big." Then I told him about the symptoms I'd been having, but otherwise probably wouldn't have even mentioned them. I was given an ultrasound test that showed tumors on both of my ovaries. Next I had blood drawn for a CA125 test (normal numbers are 0 – 35) and my test came back at 2,200. A CA125 test measures the amount of the protein (cancer antigen 125) in your blood. Certain cancers can cause CA125 to be released into the bloodstream and ovarian is one of them. Since my number was so elevated there was a very good chance that I had ovarian cancer but this couldn't actually be diagnosed until I had surgery… and I needed to have it quickly.

Within a day of getting my results from the blood test I was speaking to a surgeon and scheduling a complete hysterectomy the following week. I was told that during surgery they would be able to determine if I had cancer and if so, my surgeon asked permission from me to insert internally an interperitoneal port just under my left rib that could be used for chemo. He explained that use of this (I.P.) port would give better outcome and the time to insert it was during this initial surgery. I signed a consent form and agreed to have the I.P. port installed if necessary. I asked the surgeon if I would be able to feel the port on my side when I woke up from the surgery and he said that I would.

I spent the next three sleepless nights stressing about all that I would be going through, feeling both scared and sorry for myself.

My surgery lasted about four hours. I had a needle with an IV inserted into my spine for pain, another decision I had to make that was recommended by my surgeon beforehand, and that I had to sign for. When I began to awaken from the surgery in the recovery room I had terrible spasms in my abdomen. Apparently the needle in my spine wasn't aligned properly so it had to be adjusted. The first thing I did when I fully awoke was touch my left side and when I did I felt the lump from the I.P. port and bandages over it. I was sickened to learn that I had cancer before anyone spoke with me about it.

Recovery in the hospital was rough. I was told that I had stage 3C, grade 3, high grade, epithelial serous ovarian cancer. This is the most common type of ovarian cancer and since symptoms are so vague most cases are advanced to stage 3 or 4 before it is discovered. High grade is more treatable than low grade because although it is a more aggressive type of cancer, chemotherapy can treat it more successfully. The chemo works by killing fast growing cells (both cancerous and noncancerous cells), and high grade cancer is composed of fast growing cells.

My surgeon removed 41 lymph nodes, 33 tested positive for cancer. He also removed my appendix, omentum, scraped cancer off my bladder, and did a complete hysterectomy. The omentum is the bottom lining of the stomach.

The placement of my I.P. port required two extra incisions. I had a total of 43 metal staples holding my guts together. I couldn't tell on my own, but asked my husband to count them for me.

For pain control, the device inserted into my spine during surgery, with a pain pump attached to it, was left in place for five days. It didn't seem to work that well, but I can't imagine how much more painful it might have been without it.

On my last day in the hospital my surgeon came to visit and I asked him about my prognosis. I didn't have a roommate that day and I distinctly remember him seating himself on the edge of the empty bed next to mine. He told me that I had about a 33% chance of surviving another 5 years. But that didn't mean it would be five years without fighting the return of my cancer. He said that if the cancer returned within a year I would be given more chemotherapy of a different kind. And if the cancer waited longer than a year to return, I would have more surgery and then more chemo of the same kind I had initially (the most promising type of chemo).

It wasn't a very uplifting talk and when he left my room and I was alone, I cried my eyes out. His words were not totally unexpected because I had already looked up the type and stage of my cancer on my laptop on Wikipedia in my hospital bed, and there I found a chart with the exact same percentage for survival that he had just shared with me.

I came home after seven days in the hospital and began my mending, trying to walk as much as I could and working to get my strength back. I searched for ways to handle both the pain and the sadness. I felt much like I was wearing a suit of armor, my chest and abdominal area felt very tight and my stomach felt heavy. I often walked with my arms holding onto my stomach. I couldn't sit upright for very long without tiring. On the couch I'd wedge myself against the pillows and try to get into a comfortable position.

When I slept in bed at night I had pillows all around me and two under my head as I could only lie on my back. I tried taking Vicodin when I got home, took just one pill and had terrifying nightmares all that night. I figured I could handle the pain better than the nightmares so just took ibuprofen for the pain from then on. It didn't work so well but it helped a little. It is hard to write about what I went through even now as it brings back some bad, bad memories.

After four weeks, still feeling quite gimpy, I began my chemotherapy regime. I was to have six treatments, each three weeks apart. Two different types of chemo were to be given simultaneously, one in my I.P. port and the other in a vein in my wrist.

My oncologist didn't want to use my wrist vein for chemo as she said my veins were too small. I was scheduled for surgery to have another port placed under the skin on the right side of my upper chest. Before the outpatient surgery I was asked if I deer hunted. (From that you can

105

tell I live in prime deer hunting country!) I told them I used to hunt but hadn't for the last several years. They placed the chest port on my right side then, with a tube that goes up the neck and back down near the heart. The area where the port was inserted was sore for a few days and occasionally it still gives me a little tugging feeling. Most of the time now I don't notice it is there unless I look in the mirror.

On my first day of chemotherapy treatment my I.P. port didn't work with gravity; The I.V. liquid wouldn't flow into it. After several nurses attempted to get it flowing they gave up and gave me both chemo drugs by I.V., carboplatin and paclitaxel, in my chest port. It went slow that first time to make sure I didn't have any reactions, and all went well. The whole process took about five hours.

A friend gave me a blanket to take to the chemo room with me. She had heard from others that people often feel cold when they have infusions, and she was right. I ended up covering myself with two blankets to keep warm in-between my usual hot flashes. The hot flashes kicked in shortly after my surgery and still visit me frequently today.

When my surgeon later found out that the chemo nurses didn't use my I.P. port he was upset and said they would find a way to make it work with the next treatment. An ultrasound scan, after the insertion of dye, showed that there was a kink in the tubing in the port, a loop right below the port itself wouldn't allow the liquid to flow properly. To remedy that, at the next and all the rest of my treatments, the chemo was injected into my I.P. port with a syringe in the line by my chemo nurse, usually Michael. At the same time, I received chemo in my chest port as well, with an I.V. drip.

I want to touch more on the use of the I.P. port a little bit here. I was not fond of this port as I could feel it jutting out near the bottom of my left rib cage. It was a literal sore spot, if bumped it felt like a bruise. When the chemo was placed into the I.P. port I had to wear sweat pants because the chemo liquid literally filled up my abdominal cavity and I could see my belly expand. Talk about feeling bloated, that is an understatement. When the infusion was done my bed was tilted, feet up for 15 minutes, then head up, and then I would spend time lying on

106

each side. This was done to allow the chemo fluid to reach all over inside my guts. Afterward I had to urinate frequently and drink a lot of liquids, to flush out my system. I remember my chemo nurse, Michael, telling me when done, "Now go home and drink, drink, drink." I want to take a minute here to thank him, he saved my life. During my infusions, with Michael sitting on the edge of my bed injecting the chemo, we had some pretty decent conversations, about cancer and about life. He was always upbeat and able to answer any questions I would throw at him.

My magnesium levels were monitored with blood tests as well as my white blood cell count. When my magnesium level was low I was given an IV to build it back up along with the chemo, on the same day.

About three weeks after the first treatment my hair began to fall out in clumps when I combed it or just ran my fingers through it. I knew then it was time to cut it short to make the transition to baldness a little easier. I stood in front of the bathroom mirror and cropped it with a scissors myself and layered it around my ears, etc. I had always wore my hair longer than shoulder length so it was a strange and sad feeling to have short hair. For a few days I wore a baseball cap wherever I went to "keep my hair in place". I kept it as long as I possibly could.

Within a week of my chop job I could tell that it was time for all of my hair to go so my better half, Tom, helped me buzz it all off with the electric razor that I always gave him haircuts with. At first I felt naked, and I always felt cold. I wore stocking caps to bed at night, and covered my head with scarves during the daytime. My sister bought me a few wigs and I tried wearing them but they made my head itch and they looked like wigs. Although I appreciated my sister's kindness and attempts to help me get through this all, I was never fond of the wigs. Sometimes I felt that my hair loss bothered my sister more than me.

About two-thirds of the way through the treatments I lost my eyelashes and eyebrows as well. I found I had the need to wear more jewelry when I lost my hair. Necklaces became my friends. I felt the need to express my femininity more than normal with my hair loss as my loss of hair left me feeling "butch", and uncomfortable in public. My advice to others is not to stare at women who have lost their hair, just keep moving. We don't like it when others look at us with sad eyes, that makes it all the worse.

After a few chemo treatments I began to follow somewhat of a routine. I took steroid pills the night before the treatment and the morning of the day as well. When I returned home from the treatments I took more pills that evening and for another two days. The pills helped to stimulate my appetite and keep me from getting nauseated but they also gave me hot flashes and kept me awake at night.

The day after each treatment I returned to the clinic for a shot to boost my immunity. The shot was given in my shoulder and was not painful. It caused me to feeling achy, especially in my legs, a few days later, kind of like an achy flu and was reminiscent of growing pains in my legs when I was young. About the fourth day after my chemo I had an "ick" taste in my mouth that stayed for about three days. This took away my appetite. I ate soups, cooked asparagus, and canned salmon to get through it all. Asparagus, salmon, and plain toast with butter, were my friends.

About seven days after each treatment I began to turn a corner and regain my appetite and some energy. I was told the chemo would become harder as each treatment came and this was true. After the fourth of six treatments I became more fatigued each time than the last. And when the sixth and final treatment was finished I was a tired girl.

Some special things that helped me get through the chemo were visits from family and friends, cards in the mail, and phone calls. I was thankful that my treatments lasted over the winter season when being cooped up inside isn't all that uncommon here in Wisconsin anyway. I did try each day to get outside and walk regardless of the cool temps. Just seeing the clouds, the sparkling snow, and the bright sunshine was very uplifting.

I also began and finished making a small crazy quilt for my kids for a Christmas present using old neckties, silks and bright colored fabrics. I wedged myself into the couch and stitched my brains out every day, embroidering between all the patches as I tacked them down. Stitching up that crazy quilt helped me keep my sanity. I had the notion that I must leave something behind and that I might die any day or surely that I would die within the year.

I never missed a treatment and everything stayed on schedule until I finished the sixth and last treatment in mid-February of 2013. I asked my chemo nurse on that last day if I could ring a bell, if they had a bell to ring, because I had read online of others doing this to celebrate the end of their treatments. He looked at me a little strangely and said to just wait a minute, and then returned with a bottle of wine. It felt good to be finished with the chemo but it also left me filled with uncertainty and a bit of vulnerability because I would no longer have the support of the chemo nurses and/or the routine of weekly visits and the feeling that someone was watching over me.

About six weeks after I finished chemotherapy treatments I had my I.P. port removed surgically as an outpatient. I was quite sore for a few weeks afterward, but I mended well. The port had a long plastic tube with holes in it that ran from my left side to near my right hip. I likened it to a small irrigation system. Luckily I was put under for the surgery and don't remember a thing. I was told a port of this kind can only be used once so there was no point in keeping it any longer and I was certainly o.k. with that.

I still have my chest port today. It is considered an insurance policy by the doctors if the need arises for me to use it again. It has to be flushed with heparin once a month and that is done at my clinic. I was given a prescription for lidocaine cream to place over the port an hour before it is poked/flushed and the cream works well to numb the area. I feel no pain when it is poked or flushed. The worst part of the process is the smell of the heparin inserted into it to flush it. It almost feels like you can taste it, yuck.

The port is made of titanium and is about the size of a nickel. It is under the surface and cannot be seen but sticks up a bit and sits underneath a horizontal scar from the incision that put it in place. I have no idea how long I will keep the port but am considering its removal in 2014 if all goes well. I have heard of others keeping their ports for many years. My surgeon said some consider a port a good luck charm. Not me, I consider it a constant reminder of what I've gone through and I don't like it for that reason. I've been told though that even if it is removed, the scar it leaves behind is still a constant reminder anyway, so I'm not sure yet how long I want to leave it in.

After I finished all of my chemotherapy treatments I was given another CA125 blood test with good results. From the original 2,200 before surgery, my number came down to 14. It was such a good feeling to have a normal level. I also had a CT scan and although reading the results doesn't sound all rosy, I was told that it was unremarkable. I was expecting to be told that I was in remission after the test results but no one used that phrase, so I had to ask. The correct terminology for ovarian cancer remission is N.E.D. or "No Evidence of Disease". It doesn't mean you are cancer free but if there is any cancer left yet it is microscopic or can't be seen, so having no evidence of disease is a good thing. The word "unremarkable" is a key word that lights up the face of a cancer survivor in regards to a recent scan. I loved being unremarkable.

Two months after I finished the six chemo treatments I started feeling very stiff in the joints, especially in the hips and ankles. Whenever I would sit down for a half hour or longer, I would be so stiff when I got up that it was hard to get moving. I felt like I had aged so much and I wanted to know why I felt that way. I asked both my oncologist and my cancer surgeon and neither had an answer. They told me that chemo doesn't normally cause that, and suggested that perhaps my stiffness was from inactivity during the chemo treatments.

Five months after the chemo I developed bursitis in my hips. My right hip became sore and inflamed and I had difficulty walking for a few days. I treated myself by taking a steady dose of ibuprofen and that did the trick for the hip pain. I also had trouble with shoulder pain and have since been dealing with a frozen left shoulder. A cortisone shot and therapy helped to get it unthawed, at least partially. I took Aleve for a month for the shoulder pain and I'm not sure if this was related but the stiffness left my hips, legs, and ankles. It was a good feeling to think, even if temporary, there is a way to get relief from the stiffness.

110

And temporary it was, as after a month of not taking Aleve, the stiffness returned.

After visiting both an orthopedic doctor and a rheumatologist for the stiffness and soreness of my hips and shoulders I was diagnosed with central sensitized syndrome. It is a new name for fibromyalgia and ailments that go with it. I've learned that trauma can bring it on, so I'm taking some new meds and will hopefully conquer my aches and pains. I worry that I'll just get feeling normal and then have the cancer return again. But that is me, I can't seem to stop looking over my shoulder.

I want to mention more about the troubles I have had with hot flashes since my surgery. They began almost immediately and still bother me quite a bit, although they aren't as severe as they were a year ago. At first, right after my surgery, I would wake up at night drenched in sweat with a puddle of water on my chest. And this would happen night after night. Hot flashes would come and go throughout the day too, but always seemed worse the second half of the day, perhaps when I was becoming more tired. It's been a constant struggle and I am not allowed to take any kind of hormones to ward off the flashes because of my history of breast cancer. Now I just throw off the covers when they come at night; they still come and go daily. I guess hot flashes are minor compared to other things but at times they make me want to scream.

For me now, it's physical exams every four months with my gyn/onc surgeon and in-between those I have lab work, a CA125 blood test, and checkups with my oncologist also every four months. Alternating between the two of them, I'm seen by someone every two months. My last three blood tests showed my levels at 9.7, 12.1, and 11.3. My surgeon told me the CA125 test is not always a good indicator but when the numbers double or go higher it is cause for concern and more testing. It's a "wait and see" game, one that brings anxiety along with each test. I am now celebrating one year since finishing chemotherapy.

Sometimes I think it will get easier as time goes along, and at other times I think it only means as time goes along that there is less time left before the next battle begins for me. I'm not a gloom and doomer. It's just hard to shake the facts, the percentages, and the talk I had with my surgeon the day I left the hospital. He told me that the standard treatment for ovarian cancer has not changed in 19 years; it is still dealt with in the same way. I was pretty shocked, to think there have really been no advancements and I still wonder why. Part of the reason may be because there are so many fewer women who have ovarian in comparison to breast cancer. I sometimes feel like a very small voice crying out in a room filled with pink ribbons.

If I could make just a few prayers, one of them would be to find a cure for what fate has dealt me, but not just for myself. I am lucky that I have not yet reoccurred, as some women have no breaks in treatment. Their condition becomes chronic and chemo is a lifelong challenge that never ends. Ovarian cancer can invade the intestines, causing blockage, often resulting in a colostomy for life. It can also spread to the liver, spleen, lungs and brain. I know others with ovarian cancer that have never had a remission, had surgery about the same time I did, and are already into a second fight with more treatments. I must consider myself lucky to have had a year of chemo free life so far.

I have acquaintances that have had their ovarian cancer reoccur several times and lost their hair, faced chemo with its sickness, and uncertainty time and again. They are true fighters and advocates for ovarian cancer awareness. They are my heroes.

I think of my mother and her courage to keep battling cancer when it didn't leave her alone. She tried cobalt treatments initially, and then radiation. She had two surgeries, the radical mastectomy and the removal of most of her stomach. She did not give up. Near her life's end she was able to see two more of her grandbabies. But at the end of it all, she was not ready to go. She said she had so much more she wanted to do.

My mother's religious faith was very strong, but she was still scared. I have seen that with others. I suppose it all boils down to fear of the unknown when you are truly facing death. And you can't imagine how that really feels, until you are there yourself.

It was tragic for me to lose my mother at a young age to cancer. But I want to learn from my mother's journey the best way to cope. Perhaps I will beat the odds, and not have to fight so hard like she did. One thing is certain, she will be with me in spirit all the way, either way, and for this I can be thankful.

The trick now for me is to stay upbeat, carry on, and not let cancer ruin the rest of the life I have left and all the uncertainties I face. I need to remember to let time go slowly, appreciate every day, live life fully, and embrace others who can use help and direction with their own troubles. I hope I can live my life that way, the way we all should.

APPRECIATION

Growing up in poverty and living a simple life with few modern conveniences, in a time when most Americans did have them in the 1960s and 70s gives me some unique insights. One of the biggest gifts I've been given from the experience of my younger days is appreciation. When I moved away from my childhood home and had water on tap, electricity, indoor plumbing, a kitchen range, and so much more... well I can't ever fully express how much I appreciated every little thing.

To this day when I put a slice of bread in the toaster and don't have to worry about blowing a fuse, I'm amazed. When I turn on the faucet and feel the hot water running into the sink, I feel so very lucky.

Life is so much easier for me now than in my younger days. And yes, it is also better. And that feeling of appreciation has never left me. I will never take my life today for granted.

My young and humble lifestyle has haunted me at times in my adult life, but now I am proud of it. I am no longer ashamed. Once a lifelong neighbor told me, "You always were a backwoods kind of

113

girl, weren't you?" That is the stigma attached to me, and that's o.k. I appreciate my new "backwoods" home with modern conveniences but I will never forget my simple backwoods past.

I often regret that my mother had such a hard life and a rocky marriage. She spent twenty-seven years with my father living in that tar paper shack. If I could bring her back and trade my easy life today with her hard life I would do it in a heartbeat, just to see her smile. Whenever I compare my life to my mother's, I am filled with so much appreciation for what I have enjoyed in my own adult lifetime. That appreciation overshadows any hell I'm going through now for the most part, as it should.

OVERSHADOWED

Life is full of good times, bad times.
If we chose, we'd take the good…
And let the bad times fall between
The weathered, polished planks of wood

That pave their way above the water
Where we stand and throw a cast
And jump off swimming when it's hotter
Just to make the summer last…

A little longer, daylight hours
Summertime helps heal our souls
Sunshine, dragonflies, and flowers
Bluegills on our fishing poles.

Set that hook and sit and ponder
Bare feet dangling o'er the wood,
Remember don't be overshadowed
By the bad, and not the good.

THOUGHTS ON POSITIVE THINKING

When you have a hardship you are coping with or a major illness you are fighting, so often the words, "think positive", are thrown your way time and again. They are spoken with kindness and good intention and are often said when there is a loss for other words. I can't imagine someone confronting you in a sad situation telling you the opposite, to "think negative". Someone who tells you to "think positive" has the full intention of trying to make you strive toward your best possible outcome but there are times when I have not felt very positive about my prognosis, more times than I care to admit. So when the phrase is continually spoken it becomes an irritant. It almost makes me angry but I can't express that without sounding like I'm in a major depression. And I don't want anyone to think I am feeling that low basically because I'm not supposed to feel that low.

What I'm trying to say is that a person can't always have that "positive attitude". It's impossible, especially when you are a realist. People looking from the outside in, need to know that those suffering cannot, do not, and will not always feel positive. And people on the inside need to know that it is o.k. to feel negative from time to time, it is perfectly normal. You just can't always feel positive.

I would rather someone told me to be myself rather than to "think positive". Well wishes are always welcome, wishes of good luck, and prayers for healing, are wonderful when someone is suffering. But people need to know that they are normal when they feel down and that it is alright to cry, to feel sad, and to feel sorry for oneself. It is all part of the process of acceptance.

There is another notion that a positive attitude will help a person with a life threatening illness live longer or actually beat the disease. I firmly believe that attitude has little bearing on a person's outcome. Don't let my thoughts make you feel angry. I'm just telling you the way I feel. I don't think attitude makes that much difference, it's just that a positive attitude is taught to be the "correct" way to feel.

There is something certainly worth mentioning though about the positives of having an upbeat attitude. And that is the fact that feeling positive when one can muster up the strength to, will improve the quality of life for loved ones who surround you and the quality of the time that you have left yourself.

I have learned lessons from those who went before me. My father lost his mother at the age of 16, and went off to fight a war in foreign countries that raged on for 4 years. Even with all he went through he still had a short line full of wisdom that can apply to any trying situation, no matter how big or small it is. His line was this. "It ain't much when it's all behind you." And that is so true, especially if you can take an eraser and kind of wipe off the chalk board. Half or more than half of our stress comes from the anticipation of something we have uncertainty in the outcome of and much of the time there is nothing we can do about it. But we can make the best of the time we have left, and appreciate all that we have already experienced.

At this point I'd like to throw in the other story my father told me about his war experiences. One day in the middle of the war, he found himself in Italy, perhaps in Rome, although I'm not exactly sure, hiding in a huge underground basement of some sort. While there, he walked around and marveled at the huge assortment of large statues and sculptures all around him. They were many in number and beautiful works of art that were painstakingly carried underground in the hopes that they would be spared from the destruction of war. He looked over the art with awe and wonder, that short moment took away his fears, and he never forgot it.

It is good to focus on little things when you can't find big things to be thankful for. It is easy to find little things if you look hard enough. Be thankful for sunshine, get well cards, a phone call from a friend, a warm bed, or a bowl of homemade soup.

116

One spring day, about three months after I finished chemo, I had an experience that left me feeling touched, special, for a lack of better words. I was walking down my driveway on a very bright, sunshiny day. I noticed how the water glistened on the pond from the sun and the breeze that blew lightly across it. Out of the blue I heard a whirling, rushing sound on the water way in the distance to the southwest. As I looked in the direction of the sound I saw a whirlwind forming over the pond causing the water to fly up in a circular motion. The whirlwind was about 20 feet tall. I stopped, put up both of my arms, and out loud I challenged the whirlwind to come through me. And it did! The whirlwind immediately shifted its direction and turned directly my way. It came charging across the surface of the pond passing right through my body spraying water up and on me, and then it exited behind me.

As I turned my back to watch the magic of the whirlwind disappear, I saw leaves swirling in a circular motion in its path, until it disappeared into the woods to the northeast. I felt a rush of elation, as if a healing spirit had went through my body. I was home alone at the time so had no one to share my experience with. When my husband came home from work he walked out onto the pond dike and noticed uplifted roots and leaves blown around his blueberry plants and was puzzled with it all. I told him my story, and he believed me. Whenever I recollect my whirlwind experience I feel blessed, warm, and safe.

Our peaceful pond at home where I saw the whirlwind.

SLOWING DOWN YOUR CLOCK

A friend who lost her son to cancer said to me one day, "Tick, tock, tick, tock, goes the clock." She reminded me of how fast time goes by when you don't want it to.

I keep a list on the table where I sit daily and on it I write down all the goings-on I have to remember for the week ahead. When the week is done I throw my little reminder list in the trash. A little sadness creeps over me when I do this because I feel like I am throwing a part of my life away.

Routines remind us all of how fast life passes us by. Holidays remind us of how quickly the year has passed when we decorate the house and prepare once again for a large meal or a trip to visit family or friends far away.

When I rifle hunted during the whitetail gun deer season here for many years, we had some definite routines. Every opening morning, at the start of the season, would find me bundled in many layers of clothing with blaze orange on the outside. I would be standing in a field on my husband's great grandfather's homestead together with my husband and our hunting buddies in the dark, well before the sun rose. We'd line up single file and march with our flashlights into the woods to the south toward each of our tree stands. As we walked and watched our breath flutter in the cool air, I felt as if we did this just yesterday, even though a whole year had passed.

The key to the passing of time is to make that time pass slowly. That is what I want to do with the time I have left, I want to savor every pleasant minute. One good way is to do as Henry David Thoreau said, "Simply, simplify, simplify." That is not too hard for me as my husband has been a great teacher. He has followed that advice for most of his adult life, and for that I am grateful.

DISTRACTIONS

After the diagnosis of a life threatening illness, you learn that one way to cope with reality is to take a break from it and find positive distractions. Think about finishing old projects that you started but never had the chance to finish. Think about fulfilling goals that you always had in life but never got around to.

Distractions do a world of good in taking one's mind off unpleasant thoughts, no matter how simple they might be. When I don't have distractions or goals to work toward, I don't feel as well emotionally.

When I started chemotherapy my chemo nurse suggested planning a trip when I was done, sort of a trip splurge. I decided my goal was to fly to Maine to the northern coast and see the ocean, eat lobster, and explore nature. I chose the north coast because I wanted to avoid all the tourist trappings of the mid and lower coast of Maine. Three months after I finished chemo my husband and I made that trip. It was all that I had hoped it would be, the ultimate trip for a nature lover. I love moss for some reason, and we found huge patches of the most beautiful light green moss growing along a hiking trail near an old quarry. We saw little brooks splashing along through the woods with moss decorating all the trees.

There is something about the ocean that heals as well. Each day we watched the tides go in and out. They were amazing because of their dramatic swings, moving about 14 feet in and out, twice daily. The coast of Maine was quite a deviation from my Wisconsin backwoods routine at home.

Me on a beach in Maine

This vacation was an adventure that helped me start "living" once again. I began to look at life with a magnifying lens. If you really scrutinize the little world around you it is amazing what you can find in nature that you take for granted otherwise. Whether it be the way a drop of dew sits on a single blade of grass, or how the sunlight dances and shimmers over a body of water, or how a squirrel clambers up a tree, it's all simply amazing. Observations of nature, on a daily basis, help me slow down my ticking clock and allow me to forget the bad things.

Writing has also been a great distraction for me. I was given a few journals from family and friends to jot down my thoughts in. At first I neglected to write in them, and I'm still not faithful at utilizing the journals, but I realize how great of a distraction and good therapy writing down your thoughts can be.

This past year I decided to take photographs throughout the year of all the wild flowers that I could find growing on our property. I began taking photos in May and finished in October when the killing frosts ended the growing season. Along with a photograph of each new wild flower that bloomed, I included a description and a location of where I found them. It was a fun project for me as almost weekly new flowers appeared. I hope to encourage my future grandchildren to love wild flowers like I do, and most of all, to just notice them.

Study what you love doing. Find a way to create something special for family or friends, whether it be something simple or intricate, and then go do it. You'll feel better if you are doing something useful.

Often times, keeping busy is the key to happiness.

FLIP FLOPPING

No matter how hard I try to push aside my fear of cancer returning, with distractions, and appreciation of the little things I have all around me; friends, family, remission, I still find myself flip flopping with my emotions. I don't know what else to call it. There are times when I think I have the world by the tail and everything is going to be fine. And then a few minutes later, I suddenly feel down and out, at the bottom, and in tears.

What I have learned in regard to my flip floppy behavior is that I am normal. I need to remind myself of this, and carry on. No one can be upbeat all the time as I have mentioned before. No one can be positive 24/7. We are all human and only human.

I imagine as I go through the rest of my life, and I hope it is a very long life, that I will continue to flip flop the remainder of my days. That is just me, and I hope people can accept me for who I am, and understand.

As I mentioned when I was working on the crazy quilt for my kids for a Christmas present, I had this notion that my days would be quite short. I felt like death was knocking on my door at a moment's notice. I didn't know if the chemotherapy was going to actually work, I had to wait and see. I had doubts, so many questions filling up my mind, and much of the time I felt so much anxiety that I couldn't sleep at night.

When I first received my cancer diagnosis I would cry a lot at nighttime until I learned that was a very bad thing to do. All that crying accomplished was stuffing my nose up nice and tight and making sleep even more impossible. I then told myself, "If you're going to cry, don't cry right before bedtime." I knew in my heart that crying was silly, it was a sure way to show that I was feeling sorry for myself. It solved nothing. As time passed I put more time in between crying spells and sometimes I could go three weeks without tears, and then a bit more time would pass before I'd have another spell of tearfulness.

Now I don't cry as much but I find myself now and then having a bitter attitude, a crankiness that I have to fight to shake off. I guess you could say I'm beginning to get used to the whole deal. I still hate it all with a passion, and I'd give anything to make it all go away and have my life back, my life before cancer.

GIFTS FROM AN OAK TREE

I want to include a few excerpts from my journal written in the last few months of 2013. I still like to write in my journal out in the woods where I live, often sitting next to a favorite oak tree. I feel fortunate to have spent my married years living just a mile north of the homestead where I grew up, still surrounded by the woods and wildlife that I love so much. When I sit next to an oak tree, it never fails to bring me gifts such as solitude, peacefulness, and appreciation.

Although this is not really a letter, Aunt Susan said when you write a letter, in addition to the date, you should write down the location you are writing from... It is October 28th, 2013, and I'm sitting with my back leaning against a majestic old red oak tree on the south edge of our forty acres near Tom's Creek. This little creek that I love was named after a civil war captain and early settler of our community, Tom LaFlesh. Capt. LaFlesh left this area in 1887, moving off to northern California to search for gold. I don't think he ever found any; he probably should have stayed here.

I am soaking up the sunshine and all of nature that surrounds me today. The maples have already lost their leaves but the oak tree leaves are golden and the tamaracks are velvety. I just finished eating a granola bar I brought along in my pocket. Aunt Susan wouldn't have liked me eating a sugary snack like this, Aunt Theresa would have chuckled and said, "Go for it!", and Aunt Lydia would have ate it just before supper. (My father's three sisters, all wonderful gifts!)

What do I see in my spot here sitting on the ground amid the fallen leaves at the base of this grand old oak tree? What do I hear? I see the tree's branches reaching high up into a clear blue sky. I see the shadows created by the sun from my pen on this page. I hear crows cawing in the distance and a chickadee close by. He is not singing his "pay-day" spring song as Grandpa Adam called it, but fall time chickadee chatter. I hear a slight wind blowing though the tree tops. I see spider web threads glistening in the sunlight here and there connecting themselves between small twigs and dried up fern stems. I feel the warmth of the sun on my legs; the temp is about 50 degrees. And I hear a squirrel chattering softly.

Maybe I'll sit and look for a sign that things will be o.k. ... maybe I won't have the patience to wait that long.

It's been just over a year since I was given this journal by my sister. I haven't written in it much, maybe it's too hard, but most likely I just haven't taken the time to reflect... on paper. I've done plenty of reflecting in my mind though. Don't know if that's good or bad but I do know that's normal.

And I do know it has all been so scary, like a bad, bad dream. It takes the zip out of you, takes the fun out of things that should be fun. I think it cuts back on the good adrenalin, having cancer. Maybe that's it. It's kind of like a thief that robs you of your most precious mementoes and doesn't really want them, he just doesn't want you to have them (kind of like the thief is jealous), so he throws them away – and you can never get them back. So you try to go on living your life and act like nothing is wrong, but you miss your "stuff" that was stolen and nothing can replace it. You try to carry on and pretend you never got robbed, you never got cancer... but you did.

Then comes acceptance. It is hard but you have to accept it, and you feel cheated and sorry for yourself, over and over again. And you know that solves nothing, you know how unproductive that is... but you still feel sorry for yourself anyway.

And then you think... I'm sure not the only one. But you still feel sorry for yourself... And so it goes... You keep living your life one day at a time and trying to enjoy things, appreciating every little thing, being kind to people that you encounter as often as you can be.

But you still feel sorry for yourself... That's the whole darn problem.

124

So how can I remedy that situation?
I know that:
- *I can't get "my stuff" back from the thief who robbed me.*
- *It does no good to feel sorry for myself.*
- *I am not the only one going through this.*
- *My family and friends care about me.*

I just need to get my head on straight, buck up, chin up, laugh more, live more, do more... but wait... it looks like I want more – maybe that is the whole trouble (wanting more) when I should just be satisfied, be content, with what I already had – and if one extra little special thing is yet in store for me, I should consider it a bonus!

Yes, every day from now on is a bonus. What life I've already experienced is good enough. That's the trick!

I'm still sitting by the oak tree near Tom's Creek. The crows are still cawing and I can still hear the wind blowing through the trees. What more could I possibly need right now!

Sunday, November 10th, 2013

I'm sitting again under the red oak tree by Tom's Creek. The sun is shining and a gentle breeze is blowing from the southwest. The temperature is 44 degrees. The sunlight still makes the spider webbing glisten when the light hits it just right. It is just two weeks from opening day of gun deer season. I hear occasional gunshots in the distance from hunters sighting in their rifles. But all is very peaceful in our woods.

The sun will set shortly and promises to be colorful with scattered clouds in the horizon. I write with my leather gloves on so my penmanship is worse than normal. I'm waiting for another gift from the oak tree that I sit beneath. Perhaps its first gift was plenty. What does that say about me? I am still wanting more. That's not good; greed is not a good thing.

125

Last year at this time I sat on the dike of our pond and waited and watched the red dragon flies land on my hand and my coat. That was all the farther I could walk, from my house to the dike, after my cancer surgery. On those special days the dragonflies spelled "Victory" for me.

Today I can walk two miles. A person tends to forget how bad things were... how much progress I have made. Today the oak tree is teaching me to reflect in a positive way! It is saying to me, "Look how far you have come – enjoy today – appreciate the now – forget the past - don't dwell on the future – remember today! Live life today!"

Late fall in 2012 when dragonflies visited me by the pond

I hear the crows cawing gently. I stretch my ears to hear another flock of Sandhill cranes pass over as they migrate south. Their prehistoric voices enlighten me. A barred owl gives his "who cooks for you" call twice, far to the northwest. I wait and watch for a whitetail buck to stumble my way in his quest for a mate and then I hear the Sandhill cranes again! I cannot see them but their call is unmistakable, it's a large flock this time. The crane song is one of nature's best songs, one of my favorites. Just think, most people probably never hear a Sandhill crane their whole lives. How lucky can I be! Here comes another huge flock....... Thank you, oak tree!

Saturday, December 28, 2013

Today with temps in the 30s, the first thaw in over three weeks, my hubby and I walk back to the oak tree carting along a couple of folding chairs to sit on. We trudge through more than a foot of snow to reach my favorite spot.

I look overhead as the sun is setting and see how its rays still shine on the very top branches of the oak tree.

A squirrel makes its way from a long distance to his leafy nest directly above me high up in the oak tree. I watch the squirrel jump from tree top to tree top. At certain points he scoots down a tree to get to a prime jumping spot and reach the branches of the next tree, then he climbs back up another and over again. It is as if the squirrel has taken this route many times before and knows exactly how to get where he wants to go. The squirrel is fearless, jumping onto clusters of tiny branches at times that swing from his weight. All during his journey he carries in his mouth a cluster of something nearly the size of his head.

When the squirrel reaches the leafy nest in the oak tree he quickly climbs inside of it with the morsel still stuffed in his mouth. Then he brushes the leaves back together that he parted to make his entrance, and all is silent.

I am fascinated by the determination, precision, and fearlessness of the squirrel. I realize that since my cancer dx I am no longer afraid of many things that cross my path in my Wisconsin woods. I'm not afraid of the timber wolves or the bears. I feel no need to pack pepper spray any longer. If I can handle cancer, nothing else can scare me.

Shortly before we head back home, several mourning doves fly above us in their quest for a drink of water before the sun sets completely. The sound of their whistling wings as they pass over is music to my ears. The oak tree brings me a sense of fearlessness today, and what better gift could there be.

August 19, 2014

I've enjoyed another year of wellness since I concluded this memoir. My checkups continue every two months and in October it will be the two year anniversary of my ovarian cancer diagnosis and surgery. I have learned so much along this bumpy road I'm still travelling, but I have so much knowledge yet to gain in regard to coping.

At a checkup today with my surgeon, he asked me if I'm able to do everything I want to do. I pause now and contemplate what he meant by that as he asked me the same question the last time I saw him four months ago. My negative brain tells me that he is encouraging me to "do it all", not waste time, enjoy the chemo free time that I am now having to the fullest. But maybe that is not what he means at all.

Feeling contentment with my life and what I have done with it so far is my main goal. I do feel comfortable with my surroundings, more content perhaps than some who have never dealt with a life threatening illness. For this I am grateful.

I would rather sit in a woods surrounded by trees, ferns, and moss than any other place in the world, and I am so lucky to have nature at my doorstep. For this I feel thankful!

Yesterday I reflected back on the whirlwind that swept through me in the spring of 2013 while I stood on the driveway at my home and spread my arms out to embrace it. Perhaps it cured me or at least it gave me the strength to cope with cancer and face the world in the best way that I can. Family and friends have also helped me cope. God has always been there every time I've reached out to him and also when I did not.

The future is uncertain to everyone, not just me. We can surmise this, guess at that, but we are all in the same boat and will only know our own destiny when the time comes.

When I leave this world, and enter the next, according to Uncle Axel, it will just be like changing channels. I like his idea!

CLOSING THOUGHTS

I WANT TO LIVE LIKE A TREE

Before a tree is planted, you soak the roots. Then you dig the hole, plant the little seedling, water it thoroughly, and walk away. You hope the tree will survive, stay healthy, and grow tall.

You might mark your freshly planted tree with a stake, you might wrap it's trunk for protection, and you might put a fence around it to keep the critters from harming it.

As the tree grows you can take the stake away when it is tall enough to stand out on its own. Years later you can take the fence away when the trunk is wide enough so that nothing will harm the bark. But as it grows taller the tree can still fall victim to disease, the wind, or lightning. There is never a guarantee for sure that the tree will live the lifespan that it should.

We are the same. As children we are protected by our parents' guidance, and as adults most of us try to eat right, stay fit, and seek medical care that will help us live a long life... but there are still unforeseen circumstances that can chop us down, cause our highest branches to die, cause our leaves to fall prematurely, cause us to... die.

Although I may not live a full lifespan, I want to keep growing spiritually in the time I have left, deepen my roots, and lengthen my branches as I reach for the sky. I want to aim high, stand tall, and soak up the sunlight. I want to provide a little shade for my friends in the

130

heat of the day, make my voice heard in the wind, offer my hand and heart as a resting place for the weary. I want to live like a tree lives.

I WANT TO DIE LIKE A TREE

When a tree dies, whether it be a towering white pine struck by lightning, a young sumac debarked by the rubbing of a whitetail buck's antlers, or an aspen in its prime flooded out by a beaver dam, it doesn't disappear right away.

A dead tree still serves a purpose. It can be home to insects and small animals, a perch during daylight for hungry bald eagles, or a roost in the moonlight for a watchful owl. A dead tree can still be a thing of beauty in the midst of a sunset as it reaches up high into the sky exposing its twisted and gnarled branches.

I want to die like a tree dies. I want to linger on a while and let the memory of me, my thoughts, and smiles hang on with family and friends, and guide them on their way into the future without me.

I want to be useful even after I am gone. And when the day comes that a strong wind blows the memory of me away, toppling me to the ground like the tree… I want to slowly return to the earth and have another tree grow up in my place.

Our old home in 2013 with the addition on the north side removed

I'd like to express thanks to my brothers and sister and cousins for letting me write about them and for allowing me to write so much about me and not as much about them and still love me anyway.

I hope you can relate to my childhood experiences and also gain a bit of insight into the thoughts in the mind of a cancer survivor.

In times that we can't conquer , let us at least find a way to conquer the fear it brings with it, so that all who face it can enjoy the time they do have left.

My special tuxedo cat, Fred, came our way five years ago as a small kitten, scared to death, all alone, and always looking over his shoulder. We have a lot in common, Fred and me.

END NOTES

The time has come to send this little book I've put together about my childhood, and thoughts in regard to facing cancer and all the mind games that have accompanied it, for publishing. A year and more has come and gone since I finished this writing. My cancer journey continues after experiencing a recurrence in June of 2015 and yet another in February of 2016. I completed six months of more chemotherapy in November of 2015 and now am facing it all over again. I didn't have to have surgery again, so chemo didn't seem quite as harsh the second time without that extra trauma dumped on me right before it all. I also managed to keep some of my hair through the last series of treatments so that people don't notice over half of it is missing. This makes it a little easier to cope with the world around me as I don't get that sad look reflected toward me when I encounter strangers out in the world. People have no idea what I'm going through if they don't know me personally and that in itself makes coping a little easier. Not much, but a little!

Each time I face another battle I struggle through tears and then slowly began to accept the fact that it is not going away and try to move forward once again. I still deal with anxiety and depression which hits me often at bedtime. My husband lets me vent and is always there for me. I'm lucky to have his support and grateful every day for his friendship.

Life goes on and the clock keeps ticking. This third time the chemotherapy is really kicking my butt, it's no charm. I am afraid to ask questions yet about how much time I have left. I live with a question mark over my head and admit to thinking about it almost every minute of the day. I guess we all live with that question mark although I think mine is bigger right now! I need to remember to keep living each day with appreciation, remember that each new day is a bonus, and that what I've already had is good enough.

There is a bright spot in my world today, an extra stride in my step, and a bigger smile every time I think about it…. Tom and I are going to be grandparents to a bouncing baby boy this spring. There's an immense feeling of comfort in knowing that a part of me will carry on.

- February 2016

Dragonflies at home by the pond are still watching over me!

CONTENTMENT

In the back 20 woods… shady, mossy, and green
With soft, scented pine needles under my feet
A deer twists his neck to look at me,
While squirrels chaise each other up a tree
And a cool breeze drifts through the pines.

Summer is my favorite time to ponder
And walk on the knoll on the trails over yonder
But the maple trees know it won't be long
'Til their leaves are red, then brown, then gone
Across the creek where the big pines whisper.

The rattlesnake plantain shows itself here and there
While the mushrooms litter the pine needled floor
Of the woods I love not far from home
Where the tall ferns dance in the morning sun
And the deer's white tail waves goodbye to me.

As I walk along in this shady woods
With the pileated woodpeckers glidin' 'tween the trees,
Where the Indians camped so long ago
In summertime warmth and wintertime snow
I thank them for sharing this land with me.

For I'm just here passing my life and time
In a woods that I'll never truly own
But without a doubt, in my heart I know
As I walk in these woods, where the wintergreen grow
I belong… here.

~ Kay Moeller Scholtz

Made in the USA
Lexington, KY
20 September 2016